Honoré Daumier

A Centenary Tribute

Edited by Andrew Stasik

Published by Pratt Graphics Center,
an Extension of Pratt Institute

PRINT REVIEW is published semiannually by Pratt Graphics Center,
an extension of Pratt Institute, 160 Lexington Avenue, New York, N.Y. 10016
Subscription rate $16.50 annually.
Contents may not be reproduced without written permission of the publishers.
Address all communications, manuscripts, books for review to
Editor, PRINT REVIEW, 160 Lexington Avenue, New York, N.Y. 10016

Editor: Andrew Stasik
Editorial Consultant: Joan Ohrstrom
Design: Hermann Strohbach
Composition: David E. Seham Associates, Inc.
Printing: Braun-Brumfield, Inc.

This issue of Print Review 11
is published by the Pratt Graphics Center,
an extension of Pratt Institute,
with generous support from
Rudolf G. Wunderlich

Cover: Honoré Daumier, *Un Monsierurau Dessous*, 3 January 1841, lithograph (D. 718) (13¾ x 9¼ in.).
National Gallery of Art, Washington, D.C., Rosenwald Collection.

Contents

IN MEMORIAM
JEAN CHARLOT

Charles Baudelaire, 1865

Tribute to Daumier

He whose image we place before you
And whose art, above all,
Teaches us to laugh at ourselves,
This one, reader, is a sage.

He is a satirist, a mocker;
But the energy with which
He paints Evil and its sequel,
Proves the excellence of his heart.

His laughter is not the grimace
Of Melmoth nor of Mephistopheles
Beneath Alecto's torch.
Which burns them, but chills us.

Their laughter, alas! is
Only a sad satire of gaiety;
His shines forth, fresh and large
As a sign of his goodness.

Howard P. Vincent, *Daumier and His World*, North-
western University Press, Evanston, Ill., 1968, p. 157.

Peter Morse

Daumier's Early Lithographs

The prints of Daumier's first two active years have been often mentioned but little studied. They form an impressive body of work, showing Daumier's rapid development as an artist. They also, incidentally, tell us a great deal about the condition of France between July 1830 and August 1832. Although we study these lithographs because Daumier is a great artist, we must pay extra attention to his political subject matter in order to understand what makes him great. These prints are much more closely linked to their own time than are his genre subjects. Thus they need more explanation, so that we today can grasp the messages that were obvious to his contemporary audience. A chronological study can tie them with some accuracy to events of the day. Unsolved problems still remain, of course, subjects for future research.

In 1830, France was under the reign of King Charles X.[1] The Bourbon kings had been restored to the throne of France in 1815, following the Revolution and the years of Napoleon. Charles, already an old man, had succeeded his brother, Louis XVIII, in 1824. He was in principle an absolutist of the deepest dye and had no use for the liberties granted to the French people by the Charter of 1814. The Count de Polignac, the king's prime minister and close friend, was, if anything, of a more reactionary mind than his sovereign and had no discernible popular support in the country.

In March 1830, Charles made a speech to the National Assembly indicating that he planned to take absolute power. "If criminal manoeuvres create obstacles to my government," he said, "I shall find strength to surmount them in my resolve to maintain law and order." From

that moment on, his overthrow became certain. He was opposed both by conservative bourgeois businessmen and by liberals who hoped for the founding of a new republic. For months the newspapers predicted a coup d'état. These forces came to a final confrontation with the king at the end of July 1830.

22 July 1830. Daumier's first signed lithograph appeared prior to the "three glorious days" of the July revolution. It shows a French army grenadier loading his gun in the thick of battle. He turns and stares at a cannonball that has landed on the ground beside him. The print has a striking double meaning. On the surface, the meaning is purely historical, and it is the only meaning noted by most later commentators.[5] The soldier is a member of Napoleon's army—a legendary sort of hero to most Frenchmen. He is seen glancing at the cannonball, which has missed him by inches, and telling it with scorn: "On your way." In this sense, the work illustrates a bit of idealized history, very much in the style of Nicolas Charlet's lithographs. But there is another meaning, which becomes clear when we note that the cannonball has a fuse that is lit and burning. It is about to explode and utterly destroy the soldier. The rude caption is in the words of the artist, not the soldier. In this sense, the print is prophetic. Daumier could not have known that only a week later all France would explode, as he hoped, in the face of Charles X and his army.

La Silhouette, in which this print was published, was a weekly picture magazine, founded in 1829. Its illustrations, original lithographs on good paper in a quarto format, seldom dealt with political subjects. The editor was Emile de Girardin, who was later to

Photographs kindly supplied by the author.

achieve fame as the editor of *La Presse*, founded in 1836. The publisher was Achille Ricourt, one of Daumier's earliest employers and supporters, and the printer was lithographer Victor Ratier. The actual owner and managing director was probably Charles Philipon, whose life was to be inextricably linked with Daumier's for many years. *La Silhouette* expired at the end of 1830, shortly after the founding of *La Caricature*.[6]

25 July 1830. King Charles proclaimed a series of new ordinances, intending to put himself firmly in control of France. He dissolved the National Assembly, decreed new elections with a severely limited electorate, and ordered the total censorship of the press.

27-29 July 1830. The assembly refused to depart. A large group of newspapers published a manifesto against the king: "The rule of law is interrupted; that of force has begun." Spurred by this call, the people of Paris rose in revolution, barricading the streets and fighting both the police and the army. On 29 July, the aging General Lafayette, special hero of the liberal republicans, took over as chief of the National Guard. On 30 July, the newspapers called for Louis-Philippe, the Duke of Orléans and a fifth cousin of the king, to take over leadership of the country. The duke came to City Hall to assume his still-undefined role.

At the age of fifty-seven, Louis-Philippe was a popular hero. Though of royal blood, he had sided with the Revolution in 1789. A general at the age of eighteen, he had fought with the victorious revolutionaries at Valmy and Jemappes in 1792. During the Terror, he immigrated to America, but returned to Europe in 1800. Finding no place in Napoleon's France, he settled in England in 1815. After the Bourbon restoration, he went back to France, regained the vast Orléans family estates, and lived quietly until 1830. Though a cautious man, he proclaimed liberal principles that held great appeal to the country: free elections, freedom of the press, endorsement of the liberties granted by the Charter.

7 August 1830. The National Assembly voted to make Louis-Philippe the king. In an emotional scene, General Lafayette (who had declined the presidency of a republic because of his age) embraced Louis-Philippe on the balcony of City Hall. "*You* are the best of republics," he said. He later denied it, but the phrase stuck. This endorsement guaranteed the wide acceptance of the new king—the Bourgeois King, as he was soon to become known. One of his first acts was to restore to France the red-white-and-blue tricolor flag of the Revolution as its national ensign, in place of the white flag of the Bourbon kings.

Passe ton chemin, cochon.

Passe ton chemin, cochon.
[On your way, swine.]
H. Daumier
Lith. de Ratier
Blind-stamp: *LA SILHOUETTE/Album*[2]
Published 22 July 1830[3]
Delteil 1[4]

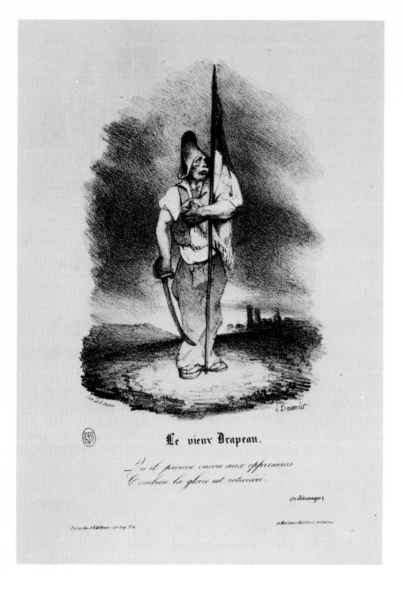

Le vieux Drapeau.
> *Qu'il prouve encore aux oppresseurs*
> *Combien la gloire est routurière.*

> *(de Béranger)*

[The Old Flag.
> May it prove again to the oppressors
> How greatly glory is of the common man.

> (by Béranger)]

h. Daumier
Lith. de V. Ratier
Paris, chez l'Editeur, r. du Coq, No. 4, et Hautcoeur
  Martinet, même rue
Deposited 11 August 1830
Delteil 2

11 August 1830. This touching print shows an old soldier, clearly a veteran of the Napoleonic campaigns, embracing the tricolor flag for which he had fought, and which had been absent from France for fifteen years. The poet and songwriter Pierre Jean de Béranger (1780-1857) was widely known and loved throughout France. During the Bourbon era, he was twice imprisoned for the political content of his songs. Daumier was particularly fond of his

poetry.[7] During the July revolution the song *Le vieux drapeau* appeared in thousands of copies, and its words and music echoed in the streets of Paris. Daumier's publisher, therefore, was capitalizing on a subject that was immediate as well as sentimental. He surely hoped to sell a large number of prints to those who had heard and sung the song a few days earlier.

11 August 1830. On the very same day, and from the same publisher, a print quite different in style and subject matter appeared. Though it is unsigned, there can be no doubt that it is also by Daumier. In dealing with a political subject rather than a romantic one, the artist used the exaggerations that are the cartoonist's trademark. Furthermore, so as not to distract from the figures, he sketched the background quickly, rather than shading it carefully, as in *Le vieux drapeau*.

The man at the left is the deposed king, Charles X. At this moment he was still in France, hiding from the wrath of the crowds. Jean Adhémar identified the other two people as the duke and duchess of Angoulême.[8] They may well have been the temporary host and hostess of the ex-king. The duchess in this print, for instance, wears the clothing of a housewife, indicating she is at home. Apparently, she is advising Charles to pretend an apology for the July Ordinances, while at the same time she hands him a sword. Charles did, in fact, try to retract his actions, but it was much too late. This print is Daumier's first caricature. The two preceding prints, though political in content, are realistic in drawing. This one shows the artist already a master of his craft. The elongated figures are ridiculous and frail. The leaning duke seems about to topple over backward, flattening both the duchess and the ex-king. The drawing is bold and sure. There is nothing superfluous in the picture.

11 August 1830. This same day also saw the appointment of Louis-Philippe's first cabinet. The ministers were: the Duke de Broglie, prime minister; Baron Louis, finance minister; Sébastiani, minister of the navy; Casimir-Périer, Laffite, and Dupin, among others, ministers without portfolio.

12 August 1830. The first legal action against a newspaper by the new government took place this day. Fifteen months later, when Charles Philipon mentioned it, actions against the press totaled 277.[9] During the preceding Bourbon era, for the most part, the publication of pictures was heavily censored, but the written press remained free. Louis-Philippe had approved the freedom of the press as one of his first royal acts: "The French people have the right to publish and print their opinions in conformity with

the laws. Censorship may never be re-established."[10] Technically, this edict held true until September 1835, in the sense that publishers could print whatever they wished without prior censorship or restraint. In actual practice, the government made life extremely difficult for newspapers by the use of other laws. Any publication that tended to "incite hate and contempt of the King's government" or that constituted "an offense against the person of the King" was subject to immediate seizure by the police. The offending matter was then brought before the attorney general, who would decide whether or not to prosecute. The editor of a newspaper and the artist of a lithograph were subject to heavy criminal penalties, as were the printer and publisher (or seller) of a lithograph. The very real possibility of prison terms gave the government considerable power of intimidation over the press. It was censorship in fact if not in law, a situation we must keep constantly in mind when looking at the political prints of Daumier or of any artist of this period.[11]

16 August 1830. Charles X boarded a ship at Cherbourg and departed for exile in Scotland.

Pleure donc feignant.
[Well, pretend you're crying.]
Unsigned
Lith. de V. Ratier
Paris, chez l'éditeur, r. du Coq, No. 4, et Hautcoeur
   Martinet, même rue
Deposited 11 August 1830
Delteil 3

Encore un petit moment, je vous en prie . . . .

Encore un petit moment, je vous en prie . . .
[Just one little moment more, I pray . . .]
Unsigned
Lith. de V. Ratier
au Magasin de Caricatures d'Aubert, Galerie Vero Dodat
Deposited 17 August 1830
Delteil 4

17 August 1830. Once we know of the fall and flight of Charles X, the main subject of this lithograph becomes clear. Less immediately obvious is the fact that the former king is rolling his eyes heavenward. His prayer for "just one little moment more" is addressed not to the straining seamen, but to God. The message is reinforced by the priest's skullcap on the back of his head. Charles had been very strongly attached to the Catholic Church and had brought its influence into many parts of the government and national life. In this, he went well beyond the prudent actions of his predecessor, Louis XVIII. The liberals, however, were frequently anticlerical. At the least, they believed in a separation of church and state along the American

model. The lithograph, therefore, is not only anti-Carlist—almost an exhausted topic at the time—it is also anticlerical, an attitude that was more important in Daumier's early works than in his later ones. It is also amusing to see that the ship waiting to carry Charles away flies the tricolor flag.

This print is the first by Daumier to be published by Aubert, soon to be the leading printseller and publisher in Paris. He was the brother-in-law of Charles Philipon, who had set him up in business in December 1829. Though Daumier probably already knew Philipon through *La Silhouette,* the connection with Aubert must have brought him into closer contact with the circle of young artists around Philipon.[12]

21 August 1830. To understand this print, we have to know that during the Paris street fighting in July, the police were among the main opponents of the mobs. The National Guard, however, made up of conscripted citizens, re-

Enfoncé les bons gendarmes.
[Finished with the good policemen.]
On the building: *Gendarmerie* [police station]
h. D.
Lith. de V. Ratier
Paris, chez l'Editeur, r. du Coq, No. 4; Hautcoeur Martinet, même rue
Deposited 21 August 1830
Delteil 5

fused in large part to fight against the people, and many of its regiments fought actively on the side of the revolution. Three weeks later, Daumier depicted three men in police uniforms lolling against a wall.[13] One peers hesitantly around the corner at the police station, which is protected by an armed guardsman. The print needs no caption to tell us that Daumier preferred the guard to the police as the protector of Paris.

The backward letter "N," a trademark of Daumier's, may be worth a mention. Throughout his life he drew it the right way on the stone, which led to a reversal in the printing. (The letter "Q" often suffered the same fate.) It could hardly have bothered him very much, for he seldom troubled to change it. It is not, of course, a failing unique to Daumier, but it is common enough in his work to catch the viewer's attention when it appears in a lithograph.

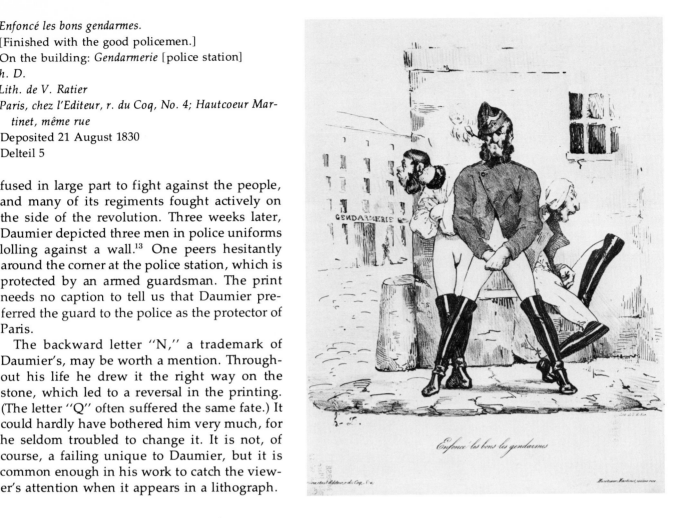

Enfoncé les bons les gendarmes

Les bons Gendarmes.
[The Good Policemen.]
Tiens bien la porte, nous sommes f . . . (The omitted word is indecent.)
[Hold the door well; we've had it.]
Unsigned
Lith. de V. Ratier
Paris chez l'Editeur, r. du Coq, No. 4; et Hautcoeur Martinet, même rue
Deposited 28 August 1830
Delteil 6

28 August 1830. This lithograph shows three policemen hiding in an attic, fearful of pursuit. The central one, disguised in a woman's bonnet and shawl, does not appear to be Charles X, as suggested by Delteil;[14] he has dark hair, and, besides, by this time, Charles had already left France. As caricatures, the figures are strong, but the subject had already become innocuous by the end of August 1830.

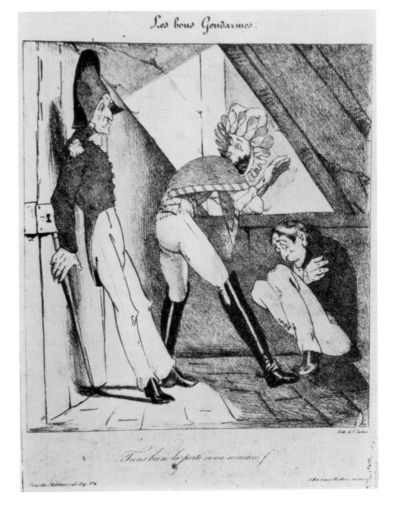

Les bons Gendarmes.

Tiens bien la porte nous sommes f

L'épicier qui n'était pas bête leur envoyait de la reglisse qui n'était pas sucrée du tout.

Il a raison l'moutard—eh oui c'est nous qu'a fait la revolution et c'est eux qui la mangent . . . (la galette).

L'épicier qui n'était pas bête leur envoyait de la reglisse qui n'était pas sucrée du tout.
[The grocer who was no fool sent them some licorice that wasn't at all sweet.]
h. Daumier
(Lith. de V. Ratier)
Paris, chez l'Editeur, rue du Coq, No. 4; Hautcoeur Martinet, même rue
No deposit date known
Delteil 7

Undated, but certainly of this period. Daumier shows us a scene from the July days. The grocer has taken up his gun and ammunition (probably his as a reserve National Guardsman) to fight against the police and the army. The two men on the ground attest the accuracy of his aim. The writing on the wall suggests that it is his own shop he is defending. The print is Daumier's tribute to the common man of Paris, who made his own revolution.

The caption, stilted in French as well as in English, has little to do with the print. (French grocers, even today, keep bits of licorice for small children.) In general, captions were composed by editors and publishers after they had seen the picture. In Daumier's case, we must keep in mind that these captions, which have become so familiar with time, have practically nothing to do with his artistic work. It is instructive to look at Daumier's lithographs while mentally blanking out the captions. Nearly all of them make excellent sense (in the context of their time) without words. Of those we have examined so far, only *Pleure donc feignant* (D. 3) would appear to need a caption. Daumier made his intentions clear. On occasion, it must be noted, he would draw people conversing and then let the editor fill in words to suit himself. This may, for instance, be the case with the two Jesuits of 4 September 1830 (see D. 9). On other occasions, an editor would suggest that a particular subject be drawn to match a preconceived idea. Whatever the case, the important point is that Daumier's pictures are to a very large extent independent of their captions.

Il a raison l'moutard—eh oui c'est nous qu'a fait la revolution et c'est eux qui la mangent . . . (la galette).
[He's right, that kid—oh yes, it's us who've made the revolution and it's them who eat it . . . (the cake).]
On the picture on the wall:
   Celui qui s'bat c'est pas celui qui mange la galette.
   [He who fights is not the one who eats the cake.]
h. Daumier
Lith de V. Ratier
Au magasin de Caricatures d'Aubert, Galerie Vero Dodat
Deposited 4 September 1830
Delteil 8

4 September 1830. This print, stylistically identical to the preceding one, shows two ragpickers looking at a lithograph on a printseller's wall. The man in the center has a bandage over one eye, clearly a wound earned in the streets in July. (One commentator notes that this man bears a striking resemblance to King Louis-Philippe.)[15] The displayed print, identified as one by Nicolas Charlet (1792-1845),[16] shows two boys talking. What they are saying, though unidentified at present, sounds like a proverb. In the context of 1830, it may also have brought to mind the expression attributed to Marie Antoinette: "Let them eat cake." The two workmen are approving the boy's sentiment: "He's right, that kid" (in the picture). The lithograph is noteworthy not only as a tribute to Charlet, but also as Daumier's first sour note, though at second hand, on the subject of the new government. What a crescendo was to arise from that simple complaint! This print was also made for the publisher Aubert, who also was Charlet's principal publisher at the time.

first acts of Charles X, in 1824, was to allow the Jesuits back to teach in the seminaries and schools of France. Criticism of any aspect of religion was censored in the newspapers.[17] To the Jesuits, therefore, the July Revolution must have appeared a disaster. A mitigating factor for them, however, was the person of André-Marie-Jean-Jacques Dupin.[18] A powerful lawyer in France during the Bourbon reign, and long known as a leading supporter of the Catholic Church, he was also a close personal friend of Louis-Philippe, Duke of Orléans. When the latter came to the throne, he appointed Dupin to his first cabinet. As a symbol of the old regime and of the church, Dupin became, not surprisingly, an early and regular target of the liberal press. If it is not already abundantly clear, the pun in the caption lies in the words "du pain" (some bread), which sounds precisely like "Dupin." The caption writer has enlarged the words to emphasize the obvious. The Jesuit is saying: "With money we will always have Dupin."

4 September 1830. Two Jesuits commiserate with one another. One turns in reassurance: "With money we will always have bread." It is a painful duty to be obliged to explain puns. The French language is nearly as well suited to such verbal humor as English. As a non-native, I can claim no special knowledge of the subject (save a lamentable predilection), and, among these lithographs, many puns may have escaped my ear and eye. One thing is sure—the chance for a pun never escaped Charles Philipon. There can be little doubt that Daumier shared his taste. In the case of this print, we need to understand several points that would have been well known to an observer in 1830. The Jesuits had been banned from public life in France during the Great Revolution. Even the restored Bourbon king, Louis XVIII, did not think it politic to let them return. But one of the

Courage, avec de l'argent nous aurons toujours Dupain.
[Courage, with money we will always have bread.]
H.D.
Lith. de Ratier
à Paris, chez l'Editeur, rue du Coq, No. 4; et Hautcoeur
  Martinet, même rue
Deposited 4 September 1830
Delteil 9

*En route mauvaise troupe! . . . c' est né dans un pays
libre et ça se vend comme Dupain.*
[Off you go, evil troop! . . . It was born in a free
country and now it sells itself like bread.]
Unsigned
Lith. de Ratier
Au Magasin de Caricatures d'Aubert Galerie Vero-dodat
Deposited 11 September 1830
Delteil 10

11 September 1830. Daumier's Jesuit print may
have had some success, for Aubert picked up
the same idea the following week. A citizen
with his trusty gun watches an army troop
marching off to re-enlist, for which there was a
cash bonus. The caption's first implication is
that the army, the enemy of the July Revolution,
sold out ("like hotcakes") to the government.
The pun implies that Dupin was as easily
bought and sold. Despite the man's faults, the
accusation of venality may be scurrilous. Dupin
was a very wealthy man, due to his success as a
lawyer. His most noted case, in fact, was when
he succeeded in getting all the confiscated Orléans estates and properties restored to the
duke, Louis-Philippe, then only recently returned from exile. That legal action alone must
have earned Dupin a huge fee.

*C'est ça de fameux cadets ils ont trouvés le moyen de
faire de la panade avec Dupain.*
[Those clever young fellows have found out how to
make mush out of bread.]
Unsigned
Lith. de V. Ratier
*A Paris Chez l'Editeur, rue du Coq No. 4, et Hautcoeur
Martinet, même rue*
Deposited 13 September 1830
Delteil 11

13 September 1830. Daumier used here the
same line technique as in the last two prints (all
three were done within ten days). His editors
probably suggested it because more impressions could be printed, and more easily, from a
stone of pure black and white, without the fine
shading of his more usual style. Two old men
are sitting on a street bench. One, pointing to a
passing Jesuit, says: "Those clever young fellows have found out how to make mush out of
Dupin." The word "mush" is the closest English equivalent that expresses the idea of
"panade," a watery sort of pudding made out of
bread and sugar.

Ya encore de l'ouvrage par là!

Ya encore de l'ouvrage par là!
[There's more work to be done over there!]
Unsigned
Lith. de V. Ratier
à Paris, chez l'éditeur, rue du Coq, No. 4; et Hautcoeur Martinet, même rue
Deposited 17 September 1830
Delteil 12

17 September 1830. This print, typical of its time, injects an entirely new and militant note into Daumier's work. Although the revolution was only six weeks old, it was already the focus of serious discontent among the people of Paris. Promises easily made—more food, more jobs, more voice in government—were not being kept. Once again workers took to the streets, not in the great numbers or with the violence of July, but in enough strength to disturb the government. Among other causes of the unrest was the beginning of a struggle by the Belgians to free themselves from a union with Holland forced on them in 1815. To the French liberals, the Belgian cause seemed a parallel to their own recent revolution. They wanted Louis-Philippe to aid the Belgians in winning a similar victory. In this lithograph, we see a band of street sweepers leaving the Tuileries Palace, the home of the king, apparently satisfied with the clean sweep they have made there. The leader points to the National Assembly as the location of their next job. The reference—to the remnant of the Bourbon regime, particularly in the Chamber of Peers—implies that the people of Paris were once more taking to the streets.[19]

Delteil states that publication of this print was refused by the censor. He does not give his source.[20] In fact, in September 1830, there were officially no censors, and the government did not have the power to refuse publication of anything in advance. That power was not assumed until September 1835. This lithograph, however, could certainly have been seized by the police at the publisher's shop. Depending on how soon the police heard of it and how fast they reacted, it might have remained on sale for many days. The attorney general must have decided against prosecution, for even an acquittal of Daumier would be well known today in the light of his subsequent fame. So, even if this print had been seized by the authorities, it would have been back in the shop of Hautcoeur and Martinet in a matter of days—and probably a better seller for having been confiscated.

Mr De-bien-au-vent.
[Mr. Fair-Wind.]
On the scrolls: *restauration 1814* [restoration 1814]
　　　　　　 restauration 1815 [restoration 1815]
　　　　　　 ambassade Angleterre 1830 [embassy
　　　　　　　　England 1830]
On the building: *Lutsworth*
H. D.
Lith. de Ratier
au Magasin de Caricatures d'Aubert Galerie Véro-dodat
Deposited 17 September 1830
Delteil 13

17 September 1830. Mr. Fair-Wind is Talleyrand (1754–1838), an authentic French hero—leader of the 1789 revolution, foreign minister first in 1797, and negotiator of the treaties that saved France from dismemberment by the Great Powers in 1814 and 1815. Louis-Philippe called him out of retirement at the age of seventy-six and asked him to be foreign minister once more. Talleyrand refused that office but accepted the ambassadorship to London. Daumier's easy-going gibe shows him leaping the English channel, a tricolor cockade in his hat, carrying documents that remind us of his support for the Bourbon monarchy in 1814 and 1815. Yes, there is another pun here. When Talleyrand was raised to the peerage by Napoleon, he was given the title Prince of Bénévent. His peer's coat is now turned inside out, and the crosier in his hand reminds us he was once a bishop.[21] At the time of the print, he was about to leave for London to negotiate a new treaty in which the Powers agreed not to intervene in each other's affairs (including the Belgian struggle).

It is interesting to see that the twenty-two-year-old Daumier, previously quite unknown, had been commissioned to do no fewer than thirteen lithographs in about a month and a half. This is two per week, a rate equal to that of his most successful years. For the beginner, it was astonishing. It seems clear that there was a market for vast quantities of prints in the turbulent days following the July Revolution. Daumier's initial success can probably be attributed much more to the character of the times than to the immediate recognition of a new master. In the next eight months, he was asked to do only nine more prints (that we now know). Today, his early lithographs, though very likely issued in quantities of hundreds, are extremely scarce, which suggests that collectors made no special effort to save them, as they would his subsequent prints, after he became famous. What did Daumier do between lithographs? In all probability he went back to graining lithographic stones for other artists, the source of the modest income he had earned for himself and his parents for some years.

Des Victimes de la Révolution.

Comme c'est amusant la politique

24 October 1830. While unrest and riot rose in the streets of Paris, Daumier had few commissions. His sole datable lithograph during this period is a lively but quite unpolitical drawing of two attractive, well-dressed young women taking the air in the gardens of the Tuileries. The men are seated around a newspaper kiosk in the background, totally absorbed in the news of the day, quite ignoring their customary pursuit of looking at young women. The girls are "victims of the revolution" because male attention has temporarily been diverted from them to the political news.

Des Victimes de la Révolution.
[Victims of the Revolution.]
Comme c'est amusant la politique.
[How amusing politics is.]
h. Daumier
Lith. de V. Ratier
Blind-stamp: *LA SILHOUETTE/Album*
Published 24 October 1830
Deltail 14

Undated. This print appears to have been unpublished. Delteil knew of only three proofs (which he does not locate). None of them has any inscription other than the artist's initials. This is the usual condition of a proof taken from the stone after the artist had finished his work, but before an editor had added a caption and the names of the printer and the publisher, and before the copyright deposit. The print is one of the few Daumier subjects lacking today in the collection of the Bibliothèque Nationale, the repository for copyright copies.

The hunchback, Mayeux, was the creation of the artist C. J. Traviès (1804-1859). Today, the employment of a hunchback as a figure of fun would appear in the worst of taste. The nineteenth century saw things differently. To viewers of that era, the surpassingly ugly character Mayeux could be laughed *at* for his pretensions and lascivious manner, and also laughed *with* for his sardonic view of the world's foolishness. Traviès, only four years Daumier's senior, had become widely known in about 1828 or 1829 for his invention of Mayeux. During that time, there were few restraints on plagiarism. Many other artists could and did use the same character in their own lithographs, even to the point of direct copying. That fact is important here because Delteil discovered, and reproduced next to this Daumier

No caption
Traviès caption: *Ah! Seductrice, tu frottes la bosse de
Mayeux.*

[Ah, Temptress, you're stroking
Mayeux's hump.]

h. D.
No printer
No publisher
No deposit date known
Delteil 15

print, another one of the same subject by a different hand and in the reverse direction.[22] Cautiously, he asked if the latter might be by Traviès (it is unsigned). A careful comparison with other Traviès prints of Mayeux shows that it is unquestionably by that artist. The print with Daumier's initials is equally clearly by Daumier. Since every part of the two compositions is identical, save for the reversal, it is inescapable that one was copied by its artist onto a lithographic stone with the other print in front of him. Would the creator of Mayeux have copied a proof by Daumier? It is inconceivable. We must necessarily conclude that Daumier copied the Traviès print. It was probably done as a speculative venture, with the hope of convincing a publisher to produce a new series of Mayeux prints with Daumier as the artist. It may date from a time a few months later than Delteil's placement of it. February 1831, near the known copyright date of the other Mayeux print by Daumier, would be appropriate. In retrospect, it is a very good thing that Daumier did not get locked into a Mayeux series in 1830 and 1831. Mayeux is not a character with whom Daumier could have been comfortable. Besides, the artist might never have produced the political prints that were to lead to fame and greatness. The subject matter of the print hardly needs discussion. It is Mayeux at his most licentious—in suitable company for such thoughts.

Late October 1830. This undated lithograph, placed in a later position in Delteil's catalogue, surely belongs here. During October, the street demonstrations grew stronger—one could even call them riots. To his credit, Louis-Philippe refused to call out the army to quell them, and several of his more conservative ministers resigned in protest. The king proved to be right, for the moment, and order was restored by the police alone. This action, however, drew a response from Daumier. Here we see Mangin, the Paris prefect of police, his policeman's hat and whip on the ground at the left, putting muzzles and leashes on three dogs, each of which wears the tricolor cockade. The dogs represent the people of Paris, the same people who had brought Louis-Philippe and his prefect of police to power in July, and who were now being muzzled by the same government. There is more than a little bitterness to the caricature, which needs no caption.

A further aid to dating is the printer's name: "Lithographed by V. Ratier." Ratier had printed all of Daumier's published prints to this point. The next ones listed by Delteil, however, are inscribed with the name of a new printer: "Delaunois, *Successor* to Ratier and Ducarme." One can hardly escape the conclusion that Ratier had either died or retired and his business had been taken over by Delaunois, who proudly noted the succession. This Ratier lithograph has to precede those printed by Delaunois.

2 November 1830. On this date, Louis-Philippe dismissed his first cabinet of ministers and appointed new ones, including, among others: Lafitte, prime minister and finance minister; Sébastiani, foreign affairs; d'Argout, navy; Soult, war; and Montalivet, interior. As a whole, this cabinet was considerably more liberal than its predecessor. In particular, Lafitte, the banker, was known to have strong republican sympathies. His appointment was a bid for favor with the newspapers and the crowds, but it failed. The naming of Lafitte to the top position was not interpreted as a yielding by the

king, but as a sellout by Lafitte. It was widely felt that the resignation and dismissal of the ministers were merely gestures toward the people, not a true change. The battle lines were being drawn.

4 November 1830. The first issue of the weekly newspaper *La Caricature* appeared on this day. This is not the place for a full history of that remarkable periodical. It is enough to say that for the next four and a half years it rattled the throne of the Bourgeois King with its satires, pictures, and puns. Consisting of four pages of text wrapped around (usually) two lithographs printed on fine paper, it combined mordant verbal satire, much of it written by Honoré de Balzac and Charles Philipon, with powerful caricatures. The political commentary appealed to opponents of the regime, while the prints were of a quality aimed at collectors of fine lithographs. With hindsight, we tend to think that Philipon recognized the genius of Daumier at first glance. It did not happen that way. Daumier's first print for *La Caricature* did not appear until more than a year after the

Nous n'avons plus besoin de vous.
[We don't need you any more.]
Unsigned
Lith. de Ratier
A Paris, chez l'Editeur, r. du Coq, No. 4; et Hautecoeur [sic] *Martinet, même rue*
No deposit date known
Delteil 19

Nous n'avons plus besoin de vous.

A Paris, chez l'Editeur, r. du Coq N° 4.   et Hautecoeur Martinet même rue

paper's founding, after the artist had been indicted for his *Gargantua*. The leading artist by far was Grandville. Others included the best lithographic artists in France: Charlet, Raffet, Bellangé, Descamps, Bouquet, Traviès, Monnier, and Gavarni, to name but a few. Daumier did not really reach a preeminent position in its pages until its last year.

The managing editor of *La Caricature* was Charles Philipon (1800-1862), who had already had contact with the young Daumier. A book should be written about Philipon and his influence on thirty years of French history, but no one has yet done it. He has been called the founder of modern journalistic caricature. He was certainly one of its greatest practitioners. His liberal and republican opinions were continually at variance with the ruling governments. He had grown up in Lyons and was trained as an artist. Apparently he had some modest independent financial means. At the age of thirty, he found his true calling as a stimulant to other, better artists and writers, although his own work in both areas is of high quality. *La Caricature* was the first and strongest platform for his views.

Pauvres moutons ah! vous avez beau faire
Toujours on vous tondra.
[Poor sheep, ah! no matter what you do you will always be sheared.]
Caricatures Politiques no. 18 [Political caricatures no. 18]
h. Daumier
Lith. de Delaunois
Au Magasin de Caricatures d'Aubert, Galerie Vero-dodat
Deposited 1 December 1830
Delteil 18

1 December 1830. This mild lithograph is a milestone in both Daumier's work and the general history of the time. So far as is known, there is no earlier caricature by any artist that directly depicts and attacks Louis-Philippe for his political actions. The king is seen shearing his sheep, the people of France, each of which wears the tricolor cockade. Two sheep dogs tend closely, dressed in army uniforms and carrying guns. A wolf in a judge's robe and hat eyes the proceedings hungrily. (Daumier was not consistent in his symbolism. In other lithographs, dogs are the people; here, they are the government forces.) The caption, which is hardly needed, contains a light pun: "toujours on vous tondra" [you will always be sheared]/ "toujours on vous tendra" [you will always be

led around]. The face of the king is a straightforward and inoffensive portrait, which may be compared with Daumier's subsequent grotesque depictions. Altogether, it is a small beginning, but coming only five months after the king's accession it must have shocked the government and the people. If the drawing is somewhat cluttered and hard to read, it may betray the artist's nervousness at breaking new ground.

Bien heureux ceux qui ont faim et soif, parcequ ils seront rassasies

Bien-heureux ceux qui ont faim et soif, parcequ'ils seront rassasiés.
[Blessed are they who hunger and thirst, for they shall be satisfied.]
h. Daumier
Lith. de Delaunois, Suc^r de Ratier et Ducarme
No publisher
Deposited 7 December 1830
Delteil 20

7 December 1830. This subject makes as much sense today as it did in 1830. The grossly fat Jesuit priest passes the starving man with a gesture and a word from the Beatitudes. At that time, anticlericalism went hand in hand with political liberalism. The alliance of the Catholic Church and the Bourbon monarchy was too close to be ignored by the opponents of the regime. The implication, of course, was that the Church had as much influence over Louis-Philippe as it did over Charles X. That proved not to be the case, however, and Daumier and other artists soon turned their fire elsewhere.

15 December 1830. The long-awaited trial of the ministers of Charles X on charges of treason before the Chamber of Peers began this day. Among those charged was the prince of Polignac, the last Bourbon prime minister and a virulent royalist.

22 December 1830. Polignac and the other ex-ministers were sentenced to life imprisonment, a punishment that enraged the people of Paris, who felt that the convicted men deserved no less than the guillotine. Riots again erupted in the streets and lasted for several days until suppressed by the army and the police.

24 December 1830. Because he refused to order the National Guard out to put down the demonstrations, General Lafayette resigned (or was fired, it is not clear) as its commander. The king replaced him with the deeply conservative Marshal Lobau.

Tout beau! tout beau, les vilains!
[Easy does it, you scoundrels!]
h. D.
Lith. de Delaunois Suc^r de Ratier et Ducarme
No publisher
No deposit date known
Delteil 16

Undated. This lithograph, of an unknown date, probably refers to the life sentences given to the Bourbon ministers. An aged peer, recognizable by his costume, is dangling a fishing line and holding a whip. The peer is not recognizable as an individual and may be a generalized portrait of the Chamber of Peers. On the line are hooked four tiny men, perhaps the convicted ministers, and the peer is teasing a pack of dogs wearing the cockade. The implication seems clear: the Chamber of Peers is teasing the Paris crowds by failing to give them what they most wanted, the death sentence. ("Throwing someone to the dogs" has the same meaning in French as in English.) The whip is a clear-cut symbol of the police, who carried the weapon, and who were active in suppressing the demonstrations. There is thus a very close agreement between the caricature and the situation, which strongly suggests that the print belongs in the last days of 1830 or in early 1831, when the issue was still current. In addition, the name of the printer, Delaunois, places this lithograph later than those printed by Ratier.[23]

Ah! tu m'appeleras Polignac!
[So! Call me Polignac, will you!]
h. Daumier
Lith. de Delaunois, Suc^r de Ratier et Ducarme
No publisher
No deposit date known
Delteil 17

Undated. Here we see a ragpicker brutally kicking his wife because she had called him an obscene name: Polignac. The print must surely date from this time, when the despised ex-minister was very much in the news. But it is more than just a street scene. The man wears a policeman's cap, and a National Guard sabre, belt, and epaulettes hang on the wall. Furthermore, the man looks remarkably like the individual in Daumier's print, *Monseigneur, s'ils persistent . . .* , of 1 June 1831 (D. 24), who is certainly General Lobau. Both portraits show a man with a receding chin and a striking turned-up nose. It seems likely that Daumier was expressing deep anger at the replacement of the hero, Lafayette, by Lobau. In effect, the artist implies, Lobau is no better than Polignac—both were men who would react violently to an insult.

Décembre 1830.

Aux petits des oiseaux il donne la pâture.

Décembre 1830.
Aux petits des oiseaux il donne la pâture.
[December 1830.]
[To baby birds he gives nourishment.]
h. Daumier
Lith. de Delaunois, Sucr de Ratier et Ducarme
Chez Aubert, Editeur du Journal la Caricature, Galerie
  Véro-Dodat
Deposited 10 January 1831
Delteil 21

10 January 1831. A bishop blesses a rich feast, while four priests gorge themselves. The caption is from *Athalie* by Racine.[24] The print may represent no more than some fat clerics at a Christmas dinner. One is struck, however, by the fact that Pope Pius VIII had died on 30 December 1830, after a reign of less than two years. His brief history gives no immediate clue to any hidden meaning in his caricature. It is also worth noting that Aubert now describes himself as the publisher of *La Caricature*. This does not mean that the print so inscribed appeared in that journal. It was merely a form of advertising both for *La Caricature* and for Aubert.[25]

January—February 1831. During these two months, there were a number of important political events that might have inspired strong responses from Daumier. Apparently no publisher saw fit to give him the opportunity. In early January, the government announced a new royal budget *(liste civile)* that included the huge sum of 18,533,500 francs for the support of the king and his family. This subject became more important later in the year, as we shall see.[26] On 25 January 1831, Russia declared war on Poland, which had risen in revolt against the Tsar at the end of November 1830. On 2 February 1831, a new pope was elected, Gregory XVI. Early in February political uprisings began in Italy, particularly in Modena and the Papal States, inspired by the July Revolution in France. On 15 February, the Carlists—the remaining partisans of a Bourbon monarchy—held a public memorial service in Paris. The people, already aroused by the Italian revolts, took to the streets in a resurgence of anti-clericalism. A number of churches and the archbishop's library were pillaged and burned.

Dépêche toi donc d'arriver! . . .
[Well, hurry up and get here!]
Cabinet de Societé
[Department of High Society]
Unsigned
Lith. de Delaunois, Suc^r de Ratier et Ducarme
*Paris, chez l'Editeur, rue du Coq No. 4; et Hautecoeur
  Martinet, même rue*
Deposited 19 February 1831
Delteil 22

19 February 1831. This Mayeux print was apparently published in its present form, for it includes the names of both printer and publisher and was deposited for copyright on this date. Though unsigned, it is unquestionably by Daumier. Like the other Mayeux print (D. 15), it was an attempt to capitalize on a popular character created by another artist. In this case, however, no identical Traviès print has been discovered, so this may be Daumier's original design. The lack of a signature might even deceive the buyer into thinking he had a Traviès print, though authorship was less important to the collector than subject matter. Daumier's two lithographs are very similar in style (but one Mayeux has hair and the other is bald), and they may indeed date from the same period.

The subject matter is simple: The young cocotte is urging Mayeux to follow her inside, and Mayeux, with a leer, is about to oblige. The sign says: "Department of High Society," a tame gibe at the government and the many fancy balls put on by Louis-Philippe. It is our loss that no publisher asked for stronger stuff from Daumier at this time.

24 February 1831. For the first time, a lithograph associated with *La Caricature* was seized by the government. Titled *Les bulles de savon* [Soap Bubbles] and drawn by Philipon himself, it was not actually a part of the journal, but was independently issued by Aubert. Initially, it was returned to the printseller, who displayed it prominently in his window, whereupon it was seized again. The attorney general decided to institute a prosecution against Philipon.[27]

13 March 1831. The moderate prime minister, Lafitte, and his cabinet resigned and were replaced by the government of Casimir-Périer, who was much more to the king's liking. ("Mr. Lafitte left the finances in bad shape," commented Philipon. "There's only one Louis left.")[28] The new ministers included Casimir-Périer, prime minister and interior minister; Sébastiani, foreign affairs; Soult, war; Barthe, justice; d'Argout, trade and public works; and de Rigny, navy. Many of these men have become familiar to us through Daumier's later caricatures. At the time, however, they drew no response from his crayon.

At the announcement of the new government, Louis-Philippe made a speech, telling of his plans to take greater personal control of the government. "The monarchy," he said, "is not powerless." To describe his government, he also used the phrase "le juste milieu"— meaning "the Happy Medium," or "the Golden Mean," or "the Middle-of-the-Road." The phrase became a sarcastic epithet in the mouths of his opponents.

16 March 1831. On this date, Daumier's father, with whom the artist lived, wrote to his landlord, who had politely requested the payment of some overdue rent. "I pray you to grant me the rest of the current month. I request this latitude because it will allow the completion of the work that has just been commissioned from my son. . . ."[29] There is no clue as to what that work might have been. There are no recorded lithographs after this date until June. Only the Mayeux print precedes it closely. Could a Mayeux series have been planned? Of course, it may have been something quite apart from lithographs. Or it could have been only a fond hope on the father's part. (In fact, the Daumier family was obliged to move its residence the following month.) But the tantalizing possibility remains that there are more Daumier lithographs yet to be identified from this period. In the fifty-four years since Delteil's catalogue

raisonné, no additional Daumier prints have been discovered from the years 1830 to 1832. Is it not, perhaps, time that a further search was made?[30]

April 1831. *La Caricature*, which had been quite easygoing in its humor in its early months, began to grow teeth. Philipon threw down his challenge at the end of the first half-year. "Our blows have struck hard and true, but we are called to higher destinies. Someday we will be the bogeyman *(croque-mitaine)* of the big infants who play under our eyes at quasi-government." A few weeks later, he noted happily: "The King subscribes to every newspaper but *La Caricature*."[31] In particular, the journal started to snap at the heels of Jean-Charles Persil, the attorney general who had begun vigorously to prosecute the press. That worthy had a name that provided rich opportunities for Philipon puns: *"Pére-Scie"* [Old Mister Saw]; "Mr. Persil complains of *persiflage*" (mockery); "Journalists prefer hemlock to parsley" *(persil)*.[32] It was a declaration of war.

23 May 1831. Philipon was brought to trial for the first time for a caricature. It was *Soap Bubbles*, the one he had drawn himself. At the time of its seizure (see 24 February 1831), he disassociated it from his newspaper, saying it was "too incorrect to be given to our subscribers." Philipon, who could be hard as nails in court, tended to be soft if there was a chance of avoiding court. He made the same sort of excuse later for Daumier's *Gargantua* and avoided personal prosecution for that lithograph. In the present case, he was acquitted.[33]

Mid-May 1831. There were further unrest and public action in Paris. During a particularly unruly demonstration in the Place Vendôme, the commander of the National Guard, Marshal Lobau, originated the basically humanitarian idea of using fire hoses to dampen the spirits of the crowd. He might have wished otherwise, for the hoses gave Philipon one of his most memorable images: to portray them as enema syringes. Soon syringe and enema jokes ran wild through the pages and prints of *La Caricature*. "When people saw the government armed with syringes, they turned their backsides."[34] Philipon personally drew a royal coat of arms with crossed syringes, one of them the sort designed for use on oneself. The syringe joke is the basis for Daumier's next two prints.

*Monseigneur s'ils persistent nous mettrons
    Paris en état de siège.*
[Your Highness, if they persist we will place Paris in
    a state of siege.]
On the syringes: *Ordre public* [Public order].
h. D.
Lith. de Delaunois
*chez Aubert, Ed[r] du journal la Caricature, Au
    Magasin de Caricatures Galerie Vero-dodat*
Deposited 1 June 1831
Delteil 24

1 June 1831. Here we see Marshal Lobau (with the upturned nose) in full regalia, with the addition of an apothecary's apron. He stands at the base of the column in the Place Vendôme with an assistant and squirts his syringe at the mob.[35] The caption writer gives us another pun. While the Marshal did not place Paris in a state of siege (though he threatened to), he is promising here that with his syringes he will place Paris "in a seated position." On the syringes is written *"ordre public,"* but it could easily be taken for *"ordure public"* (public excrement). Obviously, the inspiration for this subject came from Philipon, for it used his joke and was published by Aubert. In fact, from this time onward (in his early period), Daumier did lithographs for no other publisher.

*Monseigneur sils persistent nous mettrons Paris en état de siège.
chez Aubert Ed du journal la Caricature : Au Magasin de Caricatures Galerie Vero dodat*

Un Cauchemar,

Un Cauchemar.
[A Nightmare.]
On the stone: *récompense Nationale* [National reward]
On the scrolls: *Loi Martiale* [Martial law]
        Loi de non intervention [Law of non-
               intervention]
h. D.
Lith. de Delaunois
Aubert, Ed^r du journal la Caricature, (Au Magasin,
  Galerie Vero-dodat)
Deposited 1 June 1831
Delteil 25

1 June 1831. This print would make more sense if we could identify the individual portrayed. Unfortunately, he resembles no other caricature portrait by Daumier, nor is he in a context that makes him easy to name. He appears to be a young man, dressed as a peer and grasping a portfolio, which indicates he is a government minister. Only his blond hair, parted in the middle, is distinctive. Piled on his chest, in his nightmare, are a syringe and papers saying "Martial law" and "Law of non-intervention" (referring to the treaties with the Great Powers). The building stone ("National reward") hang-ing by a thread is a somewhat obscure refer-ence. At first, it would appear to be a govern-ment program of some sort, but none has been found by that name. There remains the possi-bility that it refers to an antigovernment carica-ture of that title. The print was described in an article by Balzac in *La Caricature*, No. 33, of 16 June 1831, and by Philipon in the same issue. It depicted a young patriot clamped in a pillory. It was so popular that Aubert removed all other prints from his walls and put up hundreds of examples of *Récompense nationale*. The artist is unfortunately not mentioned. That lithograph may be the nightmare threatening Daumier's sleeper. The press has always had a good opin-ion of its own power.

Daumier reworked this theme in February 1832 (see D. 41), much improving the composi-tion. It is a nearly unique case of such repetition in his work. Because the later print depicts Lafayette, commentators have claimed that this one does also.[36] The peerage and, of course, the nightmare were appropriate to him, but the face and the minister's portfolio make it clear that this is someone else. It remains something of a mystery—not, however, one incapable of solution.

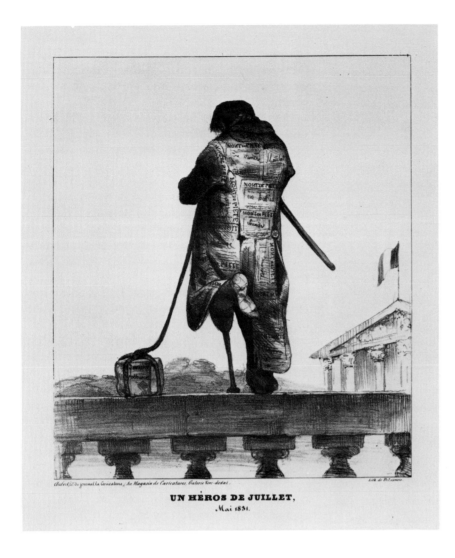

UN HÉROS DE JUILLET,/Mai 1831.
[A Hero of July,/May 1831.]
On the overcoat: *Mont de Piété* [pawnshop]
On the paving stone: *dernière ressource*
 [last resort]
Unsigned
Lith. de Delaunois
Aubert, Ed.ʳ *du journal la Caricature,*
 Au Magasin de Caricatures,
 Galerie Vero-dodat
Deposited 1 June 1831
Delteil 23

UN HÉROS DE JUILLET,
Mai 1831.

1 July 1831. The third lithograph copyrighted on the same day is a work of a totally different order. It is widely considered to be Daumier's first authentic masterpiece. Had Daumier never drawn another picture, he would be known today for this one. Here is a hero of the July Revolution, wounded for the glory of his country. A useless leg rests on a peg; his crutch is under his arm; his gray coat is made up entirely of pawn tickets for his watch, his suit, his mattress, and so on. The date is ten months after the Revolution. The hero stands poised on the bridge opposite the National Assembly, a paving stone tied to his neck with a rope. He is about to cast himself into the Seine. All the despair of the believers in the revolution is summed up in this tragic figure. Even the colorist added his touch. The sky is blue at the top, white in the middle, and sunset red at the bottom—the tricolor flag reflected in the heavens.[37] There is not a bit of wasted effort in this print, and not a bit of humor, but it is political caricature at its finest.

25 June 1831. Two Italian patriots, Menotti and Borelli, had been hanged by the duke of Modena on 26 May for their leadership of the uprising in February 1831. Before the execution, there were widespread protests in France against their condemnation and demands that French troops be sent to support this new revolution, which had been inspired by the French one. The government of Louis-Philippe did make a mild verbal protest, but took no further action. In *La Caricature*, No. 33, of 16 June there was a brutal lithograph by Raffet showing the two hanged men, with a procession of priests receding in the distance. The caption read: "Patriots of all nations, take care for yourselves!" Daumier's print is no more than a follow-up to that powerful statement. Louis-Philippe looks through a telescope at the far-away victims and utters a curt dismissal. Beside him a minister, his back turned, takes snuff. It is probably Sébastiani, minister of foreign affairs, though it little resembles Daumier's later caricatures of the man.[38] Sébastiani was known as something of a dandy, and his vanity is re-

Menotti et Borelli.
[Menotti and Borelli.]
Tant pis pour eux, nous n'y avons pas consenti.
[Too bad for them; we didn't consent to it.]
On the king's portfolio: *Affaires étrangères* [foreign affairs]
On the peer's portfolio: (illegible)
Unsigned
Lith. de Delaunois
Aubert, Ed.ʳ du journal la Caricature, Au Magasin de Caricatures Galerie Vero-dodat.
Deposited 25 June 1831
Delteil 26

flected in the elegant clothes and the snuff.[39] Daumier did not do another lithograph until October. In the meantime, things became much worse, for the country and particularly for the press.

14 July 1831. On Bastille Day, there was again violence in the streets of Paris, again suppressed with the help of Marshal Lobau's "syringes."

27 July 1831. Louis-Philippe had ill-advisedly declared the first anniversary of the revolution as a day of mourning for the patriots killed the preceding July. It became instead a day of mourning for the failure of the revolutionary ideals. Again there were riots; again they were put down by force.

Around this time, too, most artists of the liberal press seem to have stopped signing their lithographs. It was an understandable precaution, considering the growing severity with which the government was prosecuting editors, artists, publishers, and printers for their increasingly strong attacks on the government and on the person of the king. (A notable exception was Grandville, the leader of *La Caricature*'s team of artists. His style was so distinctive that it hardly mattered whether his work was signed.)

15 September 1831. There were more demonstrations and more unrest in Paris, inspired on this occasion by the fall of Warsaw to the Russians. The French saw this as yet another revolution, inspired by their own, that had been crushed by a tyrannical monarchy. During September and October, the king forced through the National Assembly a new law abolishing the right of inheritance of the nobility. This far-reaching change gave the king the opportunity to appoint new peers for life, without being troubled by their descendants, whose loyalties might lie elsewhere. In November, Louis-Philippe proceeded to name thirty-six new peers, which gave him effective control of the Chamber of Peers.

Chez Aubert, Ed.r du journal La Caricature, 1 Au Magasin, Galerie Vero-Dodat.

Lith. de Benard

Le patrouillotisme chassant le patriotisme au Palais Royal.

21 October 1831. Hostile soldiers surround a solitary citizen, who stands proudly and defiantly while rough hands grasp his collar. It is a classic confrontation between armed power and unarmed patriotism. It needs no caption. Delteil suggests that it refers back to the riots of December 1830, but there were many occasions nearer to this date that might have inspired it.[40] Actually, it makes a point more significant than any precise occasion. There is a first-state proof of this print that includes Daumier's signature, which was subsequently removed, demonstrating the prevailing caution among artists.[41] Again, the colorist has added his touch, painting the sky blue at the top and the ground pink at the bottom, to make a tricolor emblem of the whole picture.

Le patrouillotisme chassant le patriotisme au Palais Royal.
[Patroliotism hunting patriotism at the Royal Palace.]
Unsigned
Lith. de Benard
Chez Aubert, Ed.r du journal La Caricature, Au Magasin, Galerie Vero-Dodat
Deposited 21 October 1831
Delteil 28

Dieu ai-je aimé cet être là,

Dieu ai-je aimé cet être là.
[God, how I used to love that guy.]
h. Daumier
Lith. de Delaunois
chez Aubert, Ed.ʳ du journal La Caricature, Au Magasin,
Galerie Vero-Dodat
Deposited 21 October 1831
Delteil 29

21 October 1831. The second lithograph copyrighted on the same day is more gentle. A National Guardsman (the men of the guard had largely supported the revolution) stands staring at a bust of Louis-Philippe. "God, how I used to love that guy," he says. That is how any reasonable viewer would interpret the print. Then why is the boy there? He serves, of course, the purely artistic function of balancing the composition. It is possible, however, that he also serves as protection for the artist. Should the print be seized and the artist prosecuted for insulting the king, he could always claim that the guardsman was simply scolding a naughty boy, not complaining about the king. The bust, it could be said, was purely scenic decoration. (In fact, the print was not seized.) This suggestion may explain some of the weakness of the print, especially the ill-defined direction of the guardsman's attention. Such reticence is, of course, at odds with Daumier's demonstrated courage of less than two months later. But we must place him in October 1831, not in December. He had drawn the king only twice, and had never addressed a criticism directly at him. How much courage could be expected of a young artist, on the edge of poverty, with two parents to support in addition to himself? The real wonder is that Daumier soon overcame any hesitation, despite all the restraints.

14 November 1831. The indelible symbol of the pear, representing Louis-Philippe, was the accidental invention of Charles Philipon's. It began with an observation of the king's moderately pear-shaped face. From there it grew into an overwhelmingly popular fancy, even to be drawn by children on the walls of Paris. The word itself—*poire*—has the slang meaning of "nitwit," and is unusually well suited to puns. The pear could also be used by caricaturists in relative safety, for the seizure of a pear-based lithograph would be an admission by the prosecutor of the royal significance of the symbol.

The pear occurred to Philipon on the spur of the moment during a trial. He was accused of attacking the king with his lithograph of a mason plastering over the promises of the revolution.[42] "Judge me, gentlemen," he said to the jury, "if it is the king whom I attack or the power that I personify with a conventional sign. . . ." He pulled out a pencil and made four quick sketches: the first a straightforward portrait of the king, the others progressively more pear shaped. "The first resembles Louis-Philippe; the last resembles the first, and yet this last one . . . it resembles a pear!"[43] He had been speaking for at least a half hour, and he continued for as much longer, not mentioning the pear again. His initial purpose, clearly, was only to show the jury that his earlier caricature, though it looked like the king, was really not. The following week Philipon had the idea of redrawing his courtroom sketch as a lithograph. It was this lithograph, included as a supplement in *La Caricature*,[44] that caught the imagination of all France. Before that moment, there were no pear-shaped kings and no pear jokes whatever. Daumier's prints, therefore, starting with *Départ pour Lyon*, were among the first pear caricatures. They were far from the last.

The jury, unimpressed by Philipon's sketching, convicted him of offenses against the king. It was his first conviction, after ten prosecutions. He was sentenced to six months in prison and a fine of two thousand francs, the maximum under the law.[45]

October—November 1831. A series of events began in the city of Lyon, which, though they did not seriously affect the course of French history, were to drastically change the career of Honoré Daumier. In Lyon, more than forty thousand workers were employed in the silk-weaving industry, in more than eight hundred factories. In October, the government imposed new tariffs on the import of raw silk. This action led to an immediate decrease in the output of the Lyon factories, which in turn led to hundreds of workers being thrown out of work. The beginning of winter was an especially hard time to lose a job, with no money for firewood and winter clothing, never mind food. On 25 October there was a first peaceful demonstration against the tariffs, involving no more than one hundred workers. In the absence of a response, the workers again took to the streets on 10 November, still peacefully. Then, on 21 November, there began a general uprising. The army and the National Guard entered Lyon to put down the insurrection, only to retreat before the masses of people. Whole companies of the guard went over to the workers' side. Worker committees were organized to run the city and distribute food and fuel. In those days, there was a semaphore telegraph between Lyon and Paris; news of the revolt arrived in the capital without delay.

3 December 1831. On this date, a delegation from the king arrived in Lyon, ostensibly to begin negotiations with the worker committees. It was headed by the king's twenty-year-old son, Crown Prince Ferdinand Philippe, and by Marshal Soult, minister of war. The king's representatives did indeed agree to cancel the new silk tariffs. They also brought with them, however, some twenty thousand regular army troops, who effectively occupied Lyon as if it were enemy territory. The workers were disarmed and the local National Guard dissolved. Against this background, Daumier's next five prints appeared, in a crescendo of liberal bitterness that the government could not ignore.

Départ pour Lyon.
[Departure for Lyon.]
Vas poulot, et promets leur ce que je te donne.
[Go, little chick, and promise them what I'm giving
 you.]
On the pot: *Beurre* [butter]
Unsigned
No printer
No publisher
No deposit date known
Delteil 30

Early December 1831. Daumier's first version of *Départ pour Lyon* must have appeared almost at the moment the prince left Paris. It certainly was placed on sale, for it appears with title and caption and fully hand colored. It seems equally clear that the publisher (probably Aubert) expected trouble with the police, for the lithograph bears no names. It does not seem to have been submitted for copyright, for it is not in the collection of the Bibliothèque Nationale.[46]

The message is crude and simple. The king hands the prince a slice of bread covered with the butter that he has scooped out of a pot labeled "Butter." The languid prince sticks a hand in the butter as if wondering what to do with it. But a viewer would have instantly recognized the receptacle, strategically placed behind the king, as a chamber pot, the only indoor toilet known to people of the day. He is, quite obviously, giving the prince a handful of excrement, with the instruction: "Go and promise them what I'm giving you."

5 December 1831. The first print must surely have been seized shortly after it went on sale. At the same time, it must have been so successful that the publisher commissioned a replica, changed enough to placate the police. The second version, in contrast to the first, was deposited for copyright and bears the printer's name. (Hazard and Delteil noted the ghost of the letter "h" at the lower left, which the artist eradicated on sober second thought.)[47] In reproduction, the two versions appear so similar that they might be taken for two states of the same print. They are, in fact, entirely different. In all likelihood, the police seized the first stone along

Départ pour Lyon.
[Departure for Lyon.]
Vas poulot, et promets leur ce que je te donne.
[Go, little chick, and promise them what I'm giving
 you.]
Unsigned
Lith. de Delaunois
No publisher
Deposited 5 December 1831
Delteil 31

with the prints that were on sale. It is a tribute to Daumier's ability that he was able to duplicate his drawing with such precision. The only significant difference is the removal of the pot of "butter." Ironically, this deletion probably made the print even more offensive, for it left entirely to the viewer's imagination just what the sticky mass was that the king was handing to the prince. The second lithograph seems to have escaped police action.

LYON. Ils ne font q'un saut! PARIS.

LYON./PARIS.
Ils ne font q'un saut!
[They only make one jump!]
On the pot: *Compottes 1830* [Applesauce 1830]
Unsigned
Lith. de Delaporte
chez Aubert, Eeur du Jal la caricature, galerie véro dodat
Deposited 7 December 1831
Delteil 32

7 December 1831. Marshal Soult and the prince are mounted on a horse leaping from Paris to Lyon. (Their actual entry into Lyon was indeed on horseback.) The marshal is carrying a cannon, and the prince holds a pot. It is labeled "Compottes" [applesauce], which could also be read as "compost" [compost], recalling the chamber pot of the preceding print. The real offense, however, was in the caption, "They only make one *saut*" (jump), which also reads as "They only make one *sot*" (idiot). After being on sale for two to three weeks, the print was seized by the police. It was included in Daumier's trial in February 1832. The artist personally escaped prosecution for this lithograph, however, because he had not signed it. Aubert and Delaporte, whose names are on it, were acquitted.

The print was also the subject of Daumier's first mention, though not by name, in the pages of *La Caricature:*

A caricature has just appeared in Aubert's shop whose idea is as just as it is pleasant. The minister of war and the well-loved son of the king, His Royal Highness the Rainbow, are mounted on the same horse. One reads at the bottom of the drawing: "They only make one jump." Soult carries a cannon, and the little prince *(principicule)* a pot of jam *(confitures)*, doubtless to bring the workers some sweetness.[48]

Philipon had a further comment on it, and one regarding *Gargantua*, as we shall see (D. 34). Quite a few examples of this print must have been printed and sold, for the publisher had time to make two changes in the stone, correcting the caption.[49]

Arrivée à Lyon.

Entrée triomphale de l'arc-en-Ciel.

Arrivée à Lyon.
[Arrival at Lyon.]
Entrée triomphale de l'arc-en-Ciel.
[Triumphal entrance of the Rainbow.]
On the scroll: *Discours improvise* [Improvised speech]
Unsigned
Lith. de Delaunois
No publisher
Deposited 15 December 1831
Delteil 33

15 December 1831. The prince had been given the nickname "the Rainbow" (the arc in heaven) by his father. It was the stuff of caricatures. Here we see the prince arriving in Lyon, mounted on a rainbow, bearing an "improvised speech" that had been written out in advance. Beneath him hangs his cavalry saddlebag, seen in the preceding prints, but this time positioned and shaped so as to recall the chamber pot. In itself, the print is not particularly outrageous, but in the context of Daumier's other lithographs it could not be tolerated. It, too, was seized by the authorities.[50] Balzer mentions as a possible antecedent a pro-regime lithograph in which the crown prince was portrayed as the rainbow of the Old Testament, signifying good news to Noah after the Flood.[51] The use of caricature in support of the prince must have been particularly infuriating to Daumier.

15 December 1831. On the same day as the preceding work, *Gargantua* was submitted for copyright deposit. It depicts the bloated person of the king, sitting on a *chaise percé*, a chair with a hole in its seat that was used as a toilet. He is being fed with baskets of money supplied by a pitiful crowd of thin, crippled workers and carried to his gaping mouth by porters dressed as peers. At the other end, in the felicitous words of Arsène Alexandre, "he gives back through the inferior orifice of his person an avalanche. . . ."[52] The recipients, mostly peers, gather in front of the National Assembly to collect their rewards: peerages, army commissions, prefectural positions, and crosses of the Legion of Honor. Other peers reach eagerly for the money that drops from the ramp.

Gargantua, the lusty creation of François Rabelais and as familiar to Frenchmen as Swift's Gulliver is to English-speaking people, was a giant of huge appetites and equally huge excretions. Rabelais' writings were noted for containing every foul phrase in the French language and inventing new ones. The implications of *Gargantua*, therefore, were not only of immensity and insatiability, but also of extreme obscenity.

In its original context, the print was much stronger than any other contemporary attack on the king. Even the most rabid liberal artists and editors were extremely careful about the king's person. We have seen how a mild caricature earned Philipon his first conviction. Perhaps we can better visualize the impact of Daumier's print if we mentally replace Louis-Philippe with a modern American president. Despite freedom from government prosecution, caricatures of such vehemence are seldom seen today. They were far less common in 1831. The point is that *Gargantua* was very much out of the ordinary, even for its own time.

The specific target was the proposed budget for the support of the king and his family, the "civil list." The year before, the amount of eighteen million francs had been proposed. Later it was reduced to twelve million, but the sum still appeared impossibly large to the citizens. (On the first basket being carried up the ramp are the minuscule numbers "12" and "18.")

The proximate cause of Daumier's caricature was probably a short article in *La Caricature*, No. 58, of 8 December 1831, by Honoré Balzac, "Quelques articles de la liste civile." It singles out selected items from the budget and subjects them to scathing review. For the royal wine cellar, for instance, there was an allowance of 120,000 francs. It must include, wrote Balzac, some good *pots-de-vin* (pots of wine, the idiom for graft).[53] The basic idea for *Gargantua* was no doubt Philipon's, and he was probably inspired by the Balzac article.

It is interesting to note that, at the extreme right, Daumier had originally drawn a dome, representing the Royal Palace. He then attempted to scratch it out. Apparently he did not want to limit his poor taxpayers to Paris alone, but wished to include the suppressed workers of Lyon, who were still very much on people's minds.

The lithograph was not published in *La Caricature*, though many commentators have so stated. There is a slight indication that it may have been intended for such use, but it was ultimately sold only in Aubert's shop, and Philipon specifically disavowed it (29 December 1831). Perhaps he had a belated attack of caution, due to numerous recent seizures of his journal.[54] It is surprising that Daumier signed his name to a print he knew would provoke a strong reaction from the government. Surely he knew he could avoid most trouble by omitting

his signature. There is, of course, no primary evidence to resolve the dilemma. One can only imagine the artist standing in Delaporte's shop looking at the finished stone. The printer and the publisher might have turned to him with a smile: "Our names have to be on this print; how about adding yours?" And the three men would have been linked together with *Gargantua*.

29 December 1831. All three of Daumier's latest lithographs were seized by the police. The irrepressible Philipon ran the three titles together as a rude headline for his lead article in *La Caricature*:

Gargantua.
On the papers: *Préfectu(re)* [Prefecture]
        Nomination de Pairs [Nomination of peers]
        Brevet [Military commission]
h. Daumier
Lith. de Delaporte
chez Aubert galerie vero dodat
Deposited 15 December 1831
Delteil 34

Gargantua.

16th, 17th, and 18th SEIZURES MADE AT AUBERT'S.

THE RAINBOW, GARGANTUA: THE TWO MAKE ONLY ONE JUMP (idiot).

These are words that cry out to be found together. What could the Rainbow have in common with the merry son of Gargamelle?—What do they have in common? The office of a court clerk *(le greffe)* [*la greffe* means *graft*]—What? The Rainbow is placed under seal (sous les scellés)?—Why not, if the Rainbow has been arrested? . . .

As far as Gargantua is concerned, our experience has to yield to the most ingenious public prosecutor who ever discovered political blame. We have turned and returned Gargantua in every direction, and we are constrained to say that between the judge who ordered the seizure and we who do not understand the theme, one of the two is a . . . (The cruel alternative in which I find myself between the truth and a new trial will pardon this gap).

Mr. Gargantua is an enormous fellow who devours a raw budget and digests it extremely well, and who returns it immediately to the court in secretions of excellent odor in crosses, ribbons, commissions, etc., etc. . . . I am surely right, therefore, to cry to the jury: *In the long run they will make you see the resemblance there, where it will not be!* For Gargantua does not resemble Louis-Philippe; he has a head narrow at the top and wide at the bottom; he has the Bourbon nose; he has fat whiskers; but far from presenting the air of frankness, liberality, and nobility which so eminently distinguishes Louis-Philippe from all other living kings . . . , Mr. Gargantua has a repulsive face and an air of voracity that makes the coins shiver in his pocket.

Our subscribers are already familiar with the analysis of the drawing, *They only make one jump,* even though the weakness of execution of this plate, as well as *The Rainbow* and *Gargantua,* has prevented them from being destined for this journal. This caricature has departed from Mr. Aubert's window to where it even now delights fans in the indictment portfolio. Its seizure brings a dignified end to a *Caricature week.* Our publishers have suffered four prosecutions in eight days—!!![55]

This philippic is notable both for its defiance and its caution. While Philipon breathes sarcasm and anger, he also carefully disassociates himself and his newspaper from the three seized prints. They were too weak for the artistic standards of *La Caricature,* he says. Undoubtedly he was nervous, because of his own conviction. In this case, his circumspection served him well, for he was not indicted for Daumier's lithographs.

19 January 1832. Philipon was arrested and sent to jail. According to his own account, he was present when the police arrived to seize yet another issue of *La Caricature.* He apparently put up such a fuss that the police decided to take him along with his newspaper.[56] Since he had already been convicted, they had an outstanding warrant for him. He was to remain in prison (with one brief parole) until February 1833. The point is worth remembering. Though he could communicate relatively freely with his staff from his imprisonment, he could not exercise a moment-by-moment personal control over events during this critical period. The resulting weakness of direction shows in the issues of *La Caricature* over the following year.

14 January 1832. The National Assembly passed an appropriation of twelve million francs for the king's budget, along with the necessary taxes to provide the funds.

Undated. Here we see a citizen, perhaps a grocer with his apron, standing in an open square. He holds up his National Guard uniform with a "for sale" sign on it. Since March 1831, membership in the National Guard had been restricted to men who paid direct taxes. The government hoped to make it a bourgeois force, composed of small businessmen. In practice, the guard still tended to side with the crowds they were asked to suppress. In the background a drummer advances, beating the call to arms. The grocer's comment shows that he has no intention of responding. Besides, he needs to sell the uniform to pay the tax that qualified him for the guard in the first place. He has done his duty and wants no more of it.

Unlike many of Daumier's prints, this one has not been dated precisely. Delteil catalogues it in a sequence that places it vaguely between June and October 1831. Yet its style, distinctively Daumier's, seems to be somewhat later than the tightly drawn, closely shaded litho-graphs of that era. It could perhaps be a response to the final passage of the twelve-million-franc appropriation for the king. The soldier knows he will be faced with higher taxes, and he sells his uniform out of both need and disgust with the government.

There is, however, a curious bit of evidence in favor of the earlier date. In *La Caricature,* No. 47, of 22 September 1831, appears the following description of a print for sale at Aubert's: "Aubert has published several political caricatures this week. . . . One recalls the arrest of an unhappy worker who, on the Place de la Grève, sold his shirt in order to have bread." The similarities between this description and the print are striking, but so are the differences. Daumier's worker (grocer) is not selling his shirt, but his uniform; it is not to buy bread, but to pay taxes. Perhaps the writer suffered from a poor memory or wanted to disguise the subject matter for some reason. Was there a special tax imposed in September 1831? If so,

Daumier's print might be the one mentioned at that time. If not, the earlier one may have influenced his.

In addition to the matter of style, however, there is a technical point that indicates a later date. On the Daumier prints of June and October 1831, Aubert, indicating that he is the publisher of *La Caricature*, consistently has the words printed as follows: *éditeur* is abbreviated *Ed^r* with a raised "r"; *journal* is spelled out, with a small "j"; and *Caricature* has a capital "C." In contrast, on the later prints, from December 1831 on, the captions read: *éditeur* as *E^{eur}* with three raised letters, *journal* as *J^{al}* with two raised letters, and *Caricature* with a small "c." This lithograph is inscribed in the second style, which suggests, if it does not prove, that the print belongs in early 1832. It could not be later than March 1832, for Delaporte, the printer, stopped working for Aubert and *La Caricature* at that time (see 22 February 1832).

30 January 1832. Philipon (already in prison), Aubert, and Delaporte were brought to trial for a Traviès lithograph that had appeared in *La Caricature*. They were acquitted by the jury. Philipon was quite ill and his request to be transferred from prison to a hospital was soon granted. He returned to prison after the trial.[57]

Enfoncé le service/Série poli. 91
[Done with the service/Polit. series 91]
On the uniform: *a vendre pour payer l'impos* [for sale to pay the tax]
Unsigned
Lith. de Delaporte
chez Aubert, E^{eur} du J^{al} la caricature, galerie vero dodat
No deposit date known
Delteil 27

9 February 1832. This is the first of ninety-one lithographs that Daumier drew for *La Caricature* in the space of three years. Professionally, he had arrived. Though the staff of the journal was young, Daumier, not yet twenty-four, was by far the youngest. Certainly he was hired for his very real talents, but his recent notoriety played its part as well. Though he had not yet come to trial for *Gargantua*, the enormity of that offense against the king had given Daumier a considerable reputation. Philipon was quick to capitalize on it. At the same time, that fame had to be transmitted by word of mouth, for fear of further police action against the indicted artist. It is notable that Daumier's name never appears in the pages of *La Caricature* until after his arrest in August 1832. The artist who had proudly signed *Gargantua* "h. Daumier" did not put his family name on another print until his release from prison.

This lithograph shows a crowd of government ministers, many of them identifiable portraits, groveling before an empty throne to which they are tied by strings. To anyone who had seen *Gargantua*, this print would have been an obvious variation on the same theme. The minions of the king gather up the favors that

La Caricature (Journal)
(N° 67)
Pl 136

très humbles, très soumis, très obéissans
et surtout très voraces Sujets.

*très humbles, très soumis, très obéissans . . . et surtout
très voraces Sujets.*
[very humble, very submissive, very obedient . . .
and above all very voracious Subjects.]
La Caricature (Journal)/No. 67)/Pl. 136[58]
On the papers: *Pairie* [peerage], *Préfecture* [prefec-
ture], *fonds secrete* [secret fund],
avocat général [prosecutor]
h. D.
Lith. de Delaporte
On s'abonne chez Aubert, galerie véro dodat[59]
Published 9 February 1832
Delteil 40

have fallen from the throne. Though the chair
itself is empty, viewers would have chuckled at
the memory of its undignified occupant. The
new artist had given a readily recognizable calling card to the readers of *La Caricature*. The
final twist is in the word "Sujets." Only a week
earlier, the interior minister, Montalivet, had
referred in debate to the "subjects" of the king.
The French word has a stronger sense of sub-
servience than its English equivalent. People
strenuously objected to being called the king's
"subjects." It was the truth, perhaps, but an
unpalatable truth.

9 February 1832. This work was on sale at Aubert's. In London, Talleyrand was negotiating a
treaty with the other European powers to settle
the fate of Poland; the country was to be
handed over to the control of Russia. Five am-
bassadors are gathered around a conference table. The rabbit is France, submissive to the demands of the other powers. The fox is England,
the bear Russia, the gorilla Austria, and the
horse Germany.[60] In the background, we see
the Dutch dog and the Belgian turkey chained
to posts by an earlier treaty. In the foreground,
under the boot of Russia, lies the prostrate figure of Poland, which bears a striking resemblance to Grandville's figure of France in *La
France livrée aux Corbeaux* [France delivered to
the crows], published in *La Caricature*, No. 50,

13 October 1831. Daumier did not hesitate to
borrow a good idea if it served his artistic purpose.[61]

22 February 1832. Daumier, Aubert, and Delaporte were brought to trial. The proceedings
appear to have been completed in one day.
Philipon got the defendants the best defense
lawyer in Paris, Master Etienne Blanc, who had
won acquittals for Philipon on several earlier
occasions. This time Blanc's efforts were to no
avail. The three men were convicted and sentenced to stiff punishment: six months in
prison and 500 francs fine each. (They did not
plead guilty, as one authority has said.)[62]

The story of the trial, with a discreet description of the lithograph, is reported in the *Court
Gazette* of 23 February 1832:

Today the jury of the 2nd section of the Court of Assizes had three caricature matters to judge. In the first, Messrs. DELAPORTE, printer, DAUMIER, author of the lithograph, and AUBERT, print dealer, were accused of inciting hate and contempt of the King's government, and of offenses against the person of the King, in publishing a caricature entitled: Gargantua; it represents a man in whose immense mouth rests the upper part of a ladder that descends to the ground; the rungs are covered with servants engaged in wheeling sacks of coins into the maw of Gargantua, which an ill-clad and starving crowd carries to his feet; beside him are seen other persons who, placed beneath the ladder, fall avidly upon everything that falls from the wheelbarrows; finally, a sizeable group of people in fancy dress press around Gargantua's armchair and applaud ecstatically. Mr. LEGORREC, public prosecutor, undertakes the prosecution; Master E. BLANC presents the defense. The jury responds in the affirmative on all counts. The Court sentences Messrs. AUBERT, DAUMIER, AND DELAPORTE each to six months in prison and 500 francs fine.[63]

Still in effect were the provisions of the Charter of 1814, which stated that prosecutions involving the press had to be tried by jury. In the early days after the 1830 Revolution, this fact alone was enough to bring in verdicts of "not guilty." Lawyers shrewdly played to the popular sympathies of the jury. (Philipon published transcripts from three of his trials that show how effective this tactic could be in the hands of a defense attorney like Master Blanc.)[64] By the end of 1831, however, juries were becoming intimidated by the government, just at the time when criticism of it was getting harsher. The result was more and more convictions. Certainly Daumier received the best defense possible under the circumstances, thanks to Philipon, but it was not good enough for those tense times. The real surprise is that he was never again prosecuted. Perhaps his conviction had made him too much of a martyr, and the government feared popular opinion more than Daumier's lithographic crayon.

It seems evident that the courts allowed a sort of informal parole for convicted journalists. They were apparently permitted to remain at liberty despite their prison sentences as long as they were not overly offensive. The threat of

Conférence de Londres.
[London Conference.]
Signs, upper left: *Hollande* [Holland]
        upper right: *Belgique* [Belgium]
    bottom center: *Pologne* [Poland]
h. D.
Lith. de Delaporte
chez Aubert, E^{eur} du J^{al} la caricature, galerie véro dodat
Deposited 9 February 1832
Delteil 35

Conférence de Londres

prison was always present as a guarantee of reasonably good behavior. In Daumier's case, it kept him out of jail until the following August, when he was arrested (see 22 August 1832) after a particularly insulting caricature appeared in Aubert's shop. There is no evidence that Delaporte or Aubert ever went to prison. Delaporte, it seems, took the most prudent course. Although he had printed almost all of the lithographs that had appeared in *La Caricature* since its inception, his imprint disappears from those pages within a matter of days. The last Delaporte lithograph, published in the issue of 8 March 1832, was probably already "in the pipeline" at the time of his conviction. There was plenty of work for a good lithographer without getting involved in political caricature. As for Aubert, his name continues to appear without interruption in advertisements and announcements. Perhaps his relationship to the imprisoned Philipon protected him. The government may not have wanted two heroes in the same family. Oddly enough, the conviction of its celebrated artist, its publisher, and its sole printer was never mentioned in the pages of *La Caricature*.

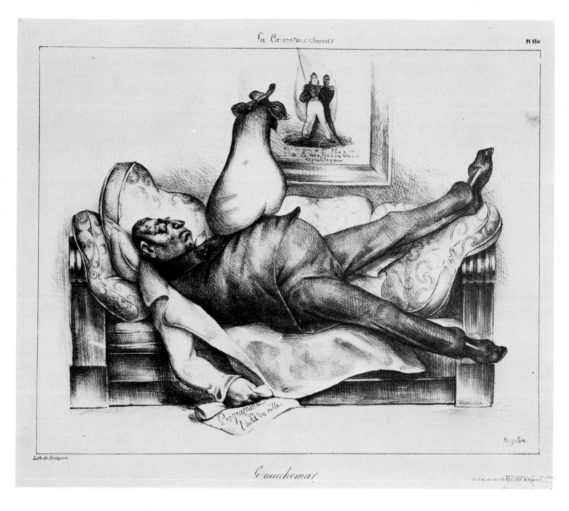

Le cauchemar.

[The nightmare.]

La Caricature (Journal)/Pl. 139

On the floor: *Programme de l'hôtel de ville* [City Hall Program]

On the picture: *La meilleure des républiques* [The best of republics]

Rogelin

Lith. de Delaporte

On s'abonne chez Aubert, galerie véro dodat

Published 23 February 1832

Delteil 41

23 February 1832. Daumier's second lithograph for *La Caricature* depicts General Lafayette suffering from the nightmare of his original endorsement of Louis-Philippe (7 August 1830). On his chest rests a huge obscene pear. In his hand is the "City Hall Program," the liberal manifesto he had given the king, and on the wall is a commemorative print of the famous embrace (perhaps a specific identifiable lithograph), which shows the two men, the tricolor flag, and the regretted words: "the best of republics." Should anyone doubt that the restless dreamer is really Lafayette, there is a little story that appeared in the next issue of *La Caricature:*

"At the session of the Chamber of Peers on the 23rd, Monsieur de Cormenin approached General Lafayette and asked him maliciously the news of his political nightmare. 'Ah! you know the new caricature,' replied the illustrious general. 'Elle est mûre, La Poire de Juillet.'"[65] This sally, with the added piquancy that the word "pear" is of the feminine gender, can be read as: "The July Pear is ripe," or as "The July Pear is all walled up." If it is not true, it ought to be.

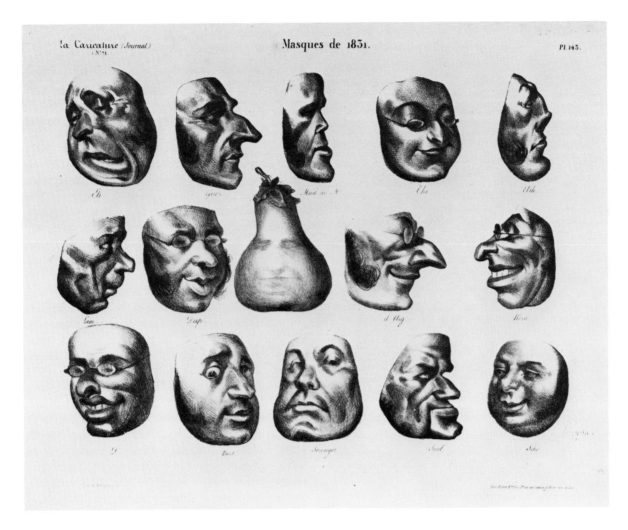

8 March 1832. This lithograph must have caused much laughter, without offending anyone too seriously. All the masks have been identified except Mr. D. at the lower left.[66] It has been suggested that Daumier based these portraits on types of facial expressions found in the lithographs of Boilly, whose *Grimaces* were published between 1823 and 1828.[67] Daumier has, in fact, precisely copied the face at the upper left (in reverse) from a Grandville lithograph.[68] Perhaps others are also copies.

It seems clear that this print was drawn just before Daumier began his remarkable series of sculpted busts upon which he based many subsequent lithographs.[69] As caricature, it is a large step beyond Daumier's earlier prints and must have won a considerable new audience for the artist.[70]

15 March 1832. Philipon emerged from prison for another trial and was found guilty for a second time. His sentence was extended by an additional six months and his fine by another two thousand francs.[71]

Masques de 1831.
[Masks of 1831.]
La Caricature (Journal)/(No. 71)/Pl. 143.
Et./Guiz./Mad. de M./Thi./Ath.
Lam./Dup./———/d'Arg./Kera.
D./Bart./Seringot./Soul./Scho.
Rogelin
Lith. de Delaporte
chez Aubert, E^eur du J^al la caricature, galerie véro dodat
Published 8 March 1832
Delteil 42

26 March 1832. The first case of cholera was discovered in Paris. This epidemic disease had swept across eastern Europe in 1831, jumping to England in early 1832. To this point, Paris had remained free of it. Within the next two months, however, it raged through the city, taking twenty thousand lives, including that of the prime minister. Business and political activity slowed almost to a halt.

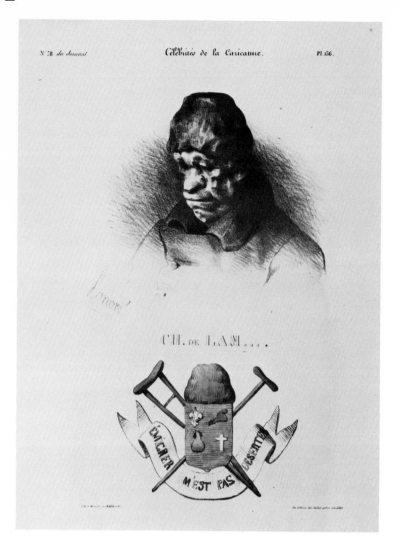

CH. de LAM . . . .
Célébrités de la Caricature./No. 78 du Journal/Pl. 156.
Emigrer n'est pas deserter. [To emigrate is not to desert.]
honoré
Lith. de Becquet, rue Childebert No. 9
On s'abonne chez Aubert, galerie véro dodat.
Published 26 April 1832
Delteil 43

26 April 1832. This print begins a series of *Celebrities of "La Caricature,"* combining a portrait with a satiric coat of arms. It had been considered by Philipon as early as January 1831, with no particular artist in mind.[72] Charles de Lameth was a peer who had sympathized with the revolution of 1789 and had voted for the abolition of the peerage. Now, at the age of eighty, he had become a staunch conservative.[73] The face is the first caricature that Daumier made from a portrait bust that he himself had modeled in clay—the first of many. The coat of arms shows Lameth's odd hairpiece and his crutches. On the shield is a fleur-de-lis, symbol of the Bourbon monarchy; a cotton cap, symbolic of the 1789 revolution; a cross, presumably denoting Charles X; and a pear. These items represent the successive governments supported by Lameth. The motto is a twisting of a phrase Lameth had recently uttered in the Chamber of Peers. There is no evident French pun in the name "LAM." Philipon apparently knew English quite well, however, and he may have expected some of his readers to know the word "lamb," and possibly "lam," as in "taking it on the lam," referring to Lameth's several flights from France.

A Aix, à Marseille, à Lyon, à Toulouse, à Bordeaux, à Angers, partout, partout, partout.

[At Aix, at Marseille, at Lyon, at Toulouse, at Bordeaux, at Antwerp, everywhere, everywhere, everywhere.]

Spoken words: *à bas l'ecrivain vendu* [down with the corrupt writer]

à bas le vendeur d'emploi [down with the job seller]

à bas l'orateur venal [down with the venal orator]

à bas le suppôt ju juste milieu [down with the henchman of the Happy Medium]

à bas le traitre [down with the traitor]

à bas l'historien renégat [down with the renegade historian]

In pockets: *Discour sur les affaires étrangers* [Speech on foreign affairs]

Discour sur le Budget [Speech on the Budget]

Vente de cet Général [Sale of this General]

honoré

Lith. de Becquet, rue Childebert No. 9

On s'abonne chez Aubert, galerie vero dodat

Deposited 12 May 1832

Delteil 36

A Aix à Marseille, à Lyon, à Toulouse, à Bordeaux, à Angers partout, partout, partout

12 May 1832. Louis Adolphe Thiers was a power in French political life for almost fifty years. In 1830, as editor of the newspaper *Le National,* he was one of the men most responsible for the overthrow of Charles X and the election of Louis-Philippe as king. In 1832, now a deputy from the town of Aix, he was appointed minister of the interior. His first act was to tour the country. This print, sold separately by Aubert,[74] gives an impression of what Thiers heard during his travels. Its immediate inspiration is undoubtedly a short paragraph in *La Caricature,* No. 79, of 3 May 1832: "Mr. Thiers, on his way to Aix, received a half portion of pandemonium *(charivari)* and a full portion of complaint. Mr. Thiers is nevertheless very fond of the sound of brass instruments."

Daumier drew more than a hundred caricatures of Thiers during their parallel careers. The prints were mainly critical, but never malevolent. Alexandre tells of an incident in about 1871: "There was a gathering of artists, writers, and politicians to which Daumier was invited. When he arrived, among the people present was Mr. Thiers. The sly little man arose, strode rapidly towards Daumier, and put out his hand, and with the petulance of a man from Marseille, complimented his compatriot. The caricaturist, who had never spared the minister of Louis-Philippe, was profoundly touched."[75]

16 May 1832. Prime Minister Casimir-Périer died of cholera. In *La Caricature,* No. 85, of 14 June 1832, Balzac (as "Eugène Morriseau") wrote: "The number of our subscribers obliges us to print the lithographs a week in advance of the next issue, and see what inconvenience it causes us: twice we have been given drawings of Casimir-Périer, and Casimir-Périer died in the interval between the printing and the publication." The caricature portraits were not published. It is tantalizing to think that one of them might have been by Daumier, in his *Celebrities* series.

24 May 1832. Charles Philipon was once more brought to trial, this time for the January seizures during which he was arrested. He won an acquittal, and made his exit with a fine flourish, selling a subscription to *La Caricature* to a member of the jury.[76]

Le Charenton Ministériel
[The Ministerial Madhouse]
La Caricature (Journal)/(No. 83)/Pl. 166, 167
Différentes monomanies des aliénés politiques.
[Different monomanias of the politically deranged.]
(There are fifteen small captions referring to individuals in the picture.)[77]
honoré
Lith. de Becquet, rue Childebert No. 9
On s'abonne chez Aubert, galerie véro dodat
Published 31 May 1832
Delteil 44

31 May 1832. In addition to what the caption writer has already given us, this print needs little explanation. Each of the political leaders is shown displaying his own particular monomania. The long horizontal format was particularly characteristic of Grandville's prints and very different from Daumier's usual close-up style. It shows that Grandville was still very much the dominant artistic influence in the pages of *La Caricature*, and Daumier still very much the newcomer. It was, however, surely a special mark of recognition for the latter to be commissioned to draw one of the special double-width plates that only occasionally appeared in the journal.

5 June 1832. General Lamarque, the great republican leader, had died; his funeral took place on this day. Philipon was given a brief parole to attend it. The occasion was the signal for a general uprising in Paris. On 7 June, Marshal Soult, minister of war, placed Paris in a state of siege that lasted for the next three weeks. Martial law gave the army license to rampage throughout the city, taking the law into its own hands. Soldiers invaded the prisons and hauled opponents of the regime before military courts. They left more than a thousand dead behind them. Philipon, in fear for his life, hid at a friend's house. *La Caricature* missed two issues, and the prior issue of 7 June was seized. (Those dated 14 and 28 June, both containing Daumier lithographs, appeared together at the end of the month. The missing date remained unfilled.)[78] There is no record of what happened to Daumier during those terrible days. He must have felt he was in danger, because of the outstanding warrant for his arrest and imprisonment. Due to the usual interval between printing and publication, it seems likely that his next two caricatures had been completed before the critical date of 5 June.

DUP . . .
La Caricature (Journal) No. 85/Pl. 171.
Plaidoyer pour/Plaidoyer contre [Argument for/
   Argument against]
Unsigned
Lith. de Becquet, rue Childebert No. 9
On s'abonne chez Aubert, galerie véro dodat
Published 14 June 1832
Delteil 45

14 June 1832. Dupin appeared in the issue bear-ing this date. Like the preceding "celebrity," his portrait was drawn with the aid of a mod-eled bust.[79] We have already made his acquaintance in the captions of Daumier's an-ticlerical lithographs of September 1830. Re-garding the caption here, it is significant that the slang word "dupe" is the same in French and English. The farcical coat of arms is sur-mounted by a lawyer's hat and topped with a weather vane. Behind it are lawyers' pleas on both sides of an issue. Emblazoned on the escutcheon is a bag of money, continuing the earlier accusations of corruption. The shoes—who knows?—perhaps they are for kicking his opponents.

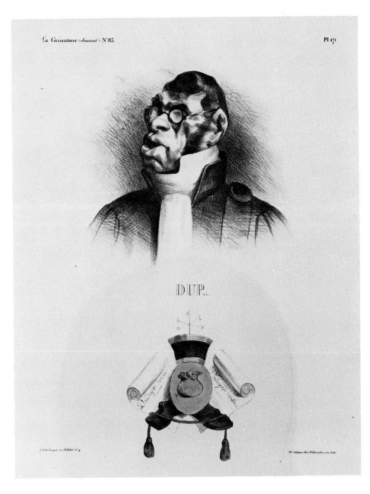

28 June 1832. Marshal Soult was the minister of war who had imposed the state of siege. His appearance at this moment is probably coinci-dental, for events suggest that Daumier had to draw this lithograph some time before the trouble started. It is very likely a portrait taken from one of the artist's growing series of sculp-ted busts. In this case, however, the bust has not survived.[80] The caption contains another punning insult. A *sou* is a five-centime piece, the smallest possible coin. At the top of the coat of arms is a cross made of a church candle and a marshal's baton. The shield has a Bourbon fleur-de-lis crossed with a tricolor ribbon in bar sinister, denoting illegitimacy. Two hats bear different cockades: one Bourbon white, the other tricolor. Behind the crosses are two bulg-ing moneybags and a minister's portfolio la-beled "WAR." In the motto, there is a pun on the word "gages," which means "wages" as well as the gage of a dueling challenge.

SOU . . .
La Caricature (Journal)/(No. 86)/Pl. 172.
On ne m'arrachera mes gages qu'avec la vie.
[You snatch away my gage only at the risk of your
   life.]
GUERRE (reversed) [War]
honoré (dimly printed in most impressions)
Lith. de Becquet, rue Childebert No. 9
On s'abonne chez Aubert, galerie véro dodat
Published 28 June 1832
Delteil 46

Le juste milieu va bien, mais les affaires ne vont pas.
[The Happy Medium fares well, but business does not.]
Caricature Politique No. 31.
[Political caricature no. 31.]
On the wall: *JOBARD./PRIX FIX.* [Jobard./set price.]
On the paper: *Debats.* [Debates.]
honoré
Lith. de Becquet, rue Childebert No. 9
chez Aubert, E.ᵉᵘʳ du J.ᵃˡ la caricature, galerie véro dodat
Deposited 14 July 1832[81]
Delteil 37

14 July 1832. Two more lithographs appeared on this date, both for Aubert's shop, not for *La Caricature*.[82] One shows a shopkeeper leaning wearily against his counter, while two clerks sleep. He wears a National Guard uniform, meaning that he had probably been called out in the streets to help put down the riots. His name, Jobard—a perfectly good French surname—has the slang meaning of "sucker." He certainly is a sucker, the artist implies, if he has been called out in the streets to support the regime of the Happy Medium, only to return to a business with no customers. He holds a paper upon which is written the word "Debates," probably referring to some ongoing sessions of the Chamber of Deputies.[83]

Nous n'avons pas la croix, nous. . . .
[We haven't got the cross. . . .]
Caricature Politique No. 32.
[Political caricature no. 32.]
honoré
Lith. de Becquet, rue childebert No. 9
chez Aubert, Eᵉᵘʳ du Jᵃˡ la caricature, galerie véro dodat
Deposited 14 July 1832
Delteil 38

14 July 1832. The second print of the same date shows two National Guardsmen complaining to each other that they have not received the cross of the Legion of Honor for their heroism in fighting the riots. *La Caricature* had commented bitterly that "crosses were distributed to the conquerors."[84] Indeed, the government had become notorious for handing out crosses in huge numbers, debasing a previously honorable decoration. (Late in life, Daumier himself was offered the same honor and turned it down.) More than fourteen thousand crosses had been awarded since the revolution two years earlier.[85] *La Caricature* had some kind words about this lithograph: "Two National Guardsmen, who are reciprocally unburdening themselves of their unhappiness at not having had their part in this great *favor*, have surely the most pleasant heads that one could ever see. We regard these two expressions as a masterpiece, and we would have given them to our subscribers if our last issue hadn't already contained a caricature about the cross of honor."[86]

19 July 1832. Two workmen and a boy struggle to hoist a huge pear to the rafters of a barn. "Hanging in effigy" is a universal concept. One may also find a much more obscene meaning, if so inclined. For once, the editor had the excellent good sense to leave this print without a caption.

26 July 1832. *La Caricature* announced the creation of a "Monthly Association" (*L'Association Mensuelle*), whose purpose was to raise funds to pay the fines imposed on the editor and artists of *La Caricature*.[87] Daumier may have been the beneficiary of this effort. Each month the association would publish a double-size lithograph by a major artist, which was available to subscribers for three francs per three months. Later, in 1834, Daumier was to draw five lithographs for the association, including some of his greatest.[88]

30 July 1832. Once again Philipon was found guilty in court. This time it was a verdict by default, because his fellow defendant, Aubert, was unable to appear due to illness. Philipon expressed his intention to appeal the conviction, and must have been successful in the end, because he spent no more time in prison after the completion of the term he was then serving.[89]

No caption
La Caricature (Journal)/(No. 89)/Pl. 179.
honoré
Lith. de Becquet, rue childebert No. 9
On s'abonne chez Aubert, galerie véro dodat
Published 19 July 1832
Delteil 47

D'ARG. . . .
La Caricature (Journal) No. 92/Pl. 188
Chacun z-a le droit. [Everyone's Entitled.]
pour avoir fait-z-un coup [?] [for having made a cut]
BEAUX-ARTS/TRAVAUX PUBLICS [Fine arts/Public
  works]
honoré
Lith. de Becquet, rue Chilbert [sic] *No. 9*
On s'abonne chez Aubert, galerie véro dodat
Published 9 August 1832
Delteil 48

9 August 1832. Here is another in the *Celebrities* series. Count d'Argout was one of Daumier's favorite targets, unquestionably because of the nose. He was also the government's censor (in fact if not in law), and was thus particularly anathema to journalists. For all that, he was apparently a gentle man and suffered his prominence in caricatures with good humor. His portrait was also done from a clay model made by Daumier.[90] In the center of the coat of arms is a paper cap, the sort commonly worn by printers, decorated with an ass's ears. The scissors are those of the censor. The portfolios are the government ministries headed by d'Argout. The "z"s in the mottos impart a nasal tone of voice. And the nose? Well. . . .[91]

22 August 1832. *Blanchisseurs* is the word for laundrymen, but it includes the connotation of bleaching or whitening *(blanc)*. That is the point of this print, and it is a strong one. The three men are Persil, the attorney general, d'Argout, the censor, and Soult, the minister of war who had recently proclaimed the state of siege.[92] They are hard at work trying to wash the red and blue colors out of the tricolor flag. The white flag, of course, was the ensign of the discredited Bourbons. The implication—that the government of Louis-Philippe was returning to the absolutism of Charles X—was a particularly sensitive one to the government that had overthrown the Bourbon monarchy. Furthermore, Marshal Soult is complaining: "This damned red sticks like blood." The same blood is seen dripping from his hand—the blood shed by the government forces during the June siege.

This lithograph, the most offensive that Daumier had done since *Gargantua*, was probably the cause of his arrest a few days later. He had overstepped, as he was bound to do, the limits of the unwritten parole that had left him at liberty. (It was a tense time in any case. The trial of some Saint-Simon socialists was due to begin the same week, and the government expected more trouble.)

Les blanchisseurs.
[The Laundrymen.]
Caricatures Politiques No. 33.
[Political caricatures no. 33.]
Le bleu s'en va mais ce diable de rouge tient comme du sang.
[The blue is coming out, but this damned red sticks like blood.]

honoré
Lith. de Becquet rue de Childebert No. 9
chez Aubert E.ᵉᵘʳ du J.ᵃˡ la caricature, galerie véro dodat
Deposited 22 August 1832
Delteil 39

23 August 1832. Pétaud was a mythological Prince of Misrule. The name also has the rude connotation of *pétard* (hind end). His fawning courtiers advance in a procession, still in the Grandville style but less so than before. Again, the principal ministers are readily identifiable. The viewer will note that the king's face had not appeared in any of Daumier's lithographs since *Gargantua* (except as barely visible features on a pear in *Masks of 1831*). The same fact held true on a wider scale. The king's face was not seen in a single lithograph in *La Caricature* (except as a pear) from 8 September 1831 to 15 August 1833.

The breakthrough was Daumier's hilarious double portrait, *1830 et 1833* (D. 66), which appeared on the latter date. Even then, there was still considerable reticence on the part of all artists to show a frontal view of the king. There are innumerable caricatures in which he is seen from the back, the side, with a hat over his eyes, and so on. There is no documentation to show a specific government mandate forbidding portrayal, but the lithographs themselves show that it was considered dangerous. This constraint is the cause of the many awkward caricatures of the faceless king.

La Cour du Roi Pétaud.
[The Court of King Pétaud.]
La Caricature (Journal) No. 94/Pl. 192, 193.
(There are ten small captions referring to individuals
  in the picture.)[93]
honoré
Lith. de Becquet, rue Childebert No. 9
On s'abonne chez Aubert, galerie véro dodat
Published 23 August 1832
Delteil 49

27 August 1832. Daumier was arrested by the police. *La Caricature* heard the news just as it was going to press. "At the moment we were writing these lines [about another print], they arrested under the eyes of his father and mother, of whom he is the sole means of support, Mr. Daumier, sentenced to six months in prison for the caricature of Gargantua. Fawning henchmen, go ahead and say it: *joy is universal.*"[94] The last bit was the recent comment of the government newspaper about a grand royal ball. After four days in a cell at the police prefecture, Daumier was officially registered in Sainte-Pélagie prison.[95]

This is an appropriate place to end the present account of Daumier's early career as an artist. During the next five months, he drew no lithographs.[96] He emerged from prison a much changed man. Before his imprisonment, Daumier showed in his lithographs the streak of bitterness, even nastiness, that we see in prints like *Gargantua* and *The Laundrymen*. In time, this tendency might have resulted in the ugliness of a James Gillray or a George Grosz. After his prison term, however, Daumier was more discriminating, more human. Alexandre made the statement in 1888 that "Up to then, the artist had only manifested the instinct of observation; after his imprisonment, he proved that he had feeling. . . ."[97] Daumier's later political caricatures are not gentle; his attacks became more effective than ever. But the wounds he inflicted were those of the rapier, not of the bludgeon. (He abandoned, for instance, the toilet humor that infected so much of French caricature of the time.) Whether he wished to be tragic or comic, Daumier could produce a scene more powerful than any known. The *Rue Transnonain* is as far ahead of the *Hero of July* as the *Legislative Belly* is ahead of *Gargantua*. Whereas the viewer would chuckle nervously at *Gargantua*, he would give a great belly laugh at the later lithograph.

I do not suggest that Daumier, in his later career, worked under any awe of the censor. His political caricatures are too strong for such doubts. But it is possible that five months in prison allowed him time for some introspection, time for him to become detached from day-to-day political aggravations, time for his essential humaneness and humanity to surface. It is hard to wish suffering on any man, but Daumier might never have been the supreme master he is without those five months in prison. His earliest prints, at least, show us what he was like before that experience, and how he came to be great.

Notes

1 General histories of France have supplied many of the details of current events. Also useful is the chronological table of events in Wolfgang Balzer, *Der junge Daumier und seine Kampfgefährten*, Dresden, 1965, pp. 246–251. This book contains what is to date the most comprehensive discussion of Daumier's early lithographs. It should also be mentioned that the five prints of 1822 and 1824, sometimes attributed to Daumier, are not considered here. I hope to offer a detailed study of them on another occasion.

2 For each print, the French caption and title are followed in order by the artist's signature (if any), the name of the lithographic printer, and the name of the printer. These inscriptions are quoted (in italics) exactly as they appear on the prints. All the printed words that appear on each print are given. Translations of the titles and captions are in brackets.

3 During this period French law required that an example of every published picture be deposited with the government. It is to some extent the equivalent of the modern copyright deposit. The prints were then marked with the date of deposit. Many of these copyright prints are now to be found in the Cabinet des Estampes of the Bibliothèque Nationale in Paris. Between 1913 and 1923, Jean Laran, the curator of prints, recorded the deposit dates of Daumier's lithographs in the collection (see Raymond Escholier, *Daumier: Peintre et lithographe*, Paris, 1923, p. 17, note 1). These dates were cited by Delteil (see note 4) and are the basis of modern Daumier scholarship. When a print was published in a dated periodical, the deposit date is usually the same as the publication date.

4 The standard catalogue raisonné of Daumier's lithographs is Loys Delteil, *Le peintre-graveur illustré: Honoré Daumier*, 11 vols., Paris, 1925–1926 (the index volume is dated 1930). Each print is numbered and arranged in a modified chronological sequence. The pages are unnumbered, so a reference to this work will be to the *print* number. *Le peintre-graveur* was preceded by N.-A. Hazard and Loys Delteil, *Catalogue raisonné de l'oeuvre lithographié de Honoré Daumier*, Orrouy (Oise), 1903. Though superseded by the later work, this catalogue remains useful for its descriptions of the print subjects and its notes on attributed prints. Delteil's contribution to Daumier scholarship deserves the most generous possible acknowledgment.

5 See, for instance, Arsène Alexandre, *Honoré Daumier: L'Homme et l'oeuvre*, Paris, 1888, p. 27. This book is the foundation of all Daumier biography.

6 *La Caricature*, No. 12, 20 January 1831. In *La Caricature*, No. 66, 2 February 1832, Philipon speaks of "*La Silhouette*, which I founded."

7 Oliver Larkin, *Daumier: Man of His Time*, New York, 1966, p. 5, cites Daumier's own word that he loved Béranger, but gives no source.

8 Jean Adhémar and Jacques Lethève, *Inventaire du fonds français après 1800*, Paris, Bibliothèque Nationale, 1953, V, p. 448.

9 *La Caricature*, No. 55, 17 November 1831.

10 J. P. T. Bury, *France 1814–1940*, London, 1969, p. 307, citing Article 7 of the law of 7 August 1830.

11 A good general history of press control in France from 1814 to 1835 may be found in Edwin de T. Bechtel, *Freedom of the Press and L'Association Mensuelle: Philipon versus Louis-Philippe*, New York, 1952. There is also a useful tabulation of the changing press-control laws in André Jardin and André-Jean Tudesq, *La France des notables: L'Evolution générale 1815–1848*, Paris, 1973, pp. 226–227.

12 On Aubert, see Jean Adhémar, *Honoré Daumier*, Paris, 1954, p. 72. This very valuable study should not be confused with idem, *Honoré Daumier: Drawings and Watercolors*, New York, 1954, which has only the briefest text. "Galerie Véro Dodat," by the way, was Aubert's address. The word "galerie" means a covered arcade. The shop is seen in a Traviès print in *La Caricature*, No. 60, 22 December 1831.

13 Hazard and Delteil, p. 52, have identified the uniforms as those of the police. For comparison, it is worth noting that at this time the Paris police numbered 1,500, the army garrison near the city 30,000, and the Paris National Guard 80,000. These numbers will give an idea of the relative strength of the forces the government had at its disposal, and their relative prominence in Daumier's prints. See William L. Langer, *Political and Social Upheaval 1832–1852*, New York, 1969, p. 82.

14 Delteil, no. 6.

15 Escholier, 1923, p. 21. Escholier also wrote *Daumier*, Paris [1913], *Daumier: 1808–1879*, Paris, 1930, and *Daumier et son monde*, Nancy, 1965. The four books have much of their text in common, but there are enough differences in the additions and deletions to make all four volumes useful to the student of Daumier. The illustrations in each are entirely different.

16 Noted by Delteil, no. 8, who refers to lithograph no. 662 in J. F. de la Combe, *Charlet: Description raisonné de son oeuvre lithographique*, Paris, 1856. The actual caption is slightly different from what Daumier wrote: *Ceux-là qui se bat . . . pour la galette, c'est pas celui là qui la mange* [Those who fight for the cake are not the ones who eat it]. The sense remains the same.

17 Bechtel, p. 19. Champfleury makes an obscure reference to this print as an "allusion to the affair of the Jesuits of Saint-Acheul" (*Catalogue de l'oeuvre lithographié et gravé de H. Daumier*, Paris, 1878, p. 5).

18 See Daumier's 1832 caricature of Dupin (D. 45).

19 At this time, the National Assembly was made up of two legislative houses: the Chamber of Deputies, elected by a severely restricted body of voters (less than one percent of the population) that consisted of men who owned more than a certain amount of property, and the Chamber of Peers, made up of those nobles appointed by a king or emperor, and after them their descendants.

20 Delteil, no. 12.

21 *Hommage à Honoré Daumier* (exh. cat.), Château de Blois, Paris, 1968, no. 5, p. 33.

22 Delteil, no. 15.

23 It is only fair to point out that this print also has some parallels with the situation in early November 1830. Louis-Philippe had just dismissed one cabinet and replaced it with a new one, nominally more liberal. The peer may be throwing the old cabinet ministers to the dogs. The historical facts, however, do not support the interpretation of the earlier date as well as they do the later one. The Chamber of Peers, for instance, seems to have had little to do with the earlier situation.

24 Alexandre, p. 29. I regret I do not know the exact context of the quotation. It might be helpful in understanding the print.

25 The reader who is unfamiliar with French may wish to note some occasionally confusing translations. The managing editor or director of a periodical is *le gérant,* as was Philipon for *La Caricature.* The city editor is *rédacteur en chef.* The publisher is *l'éditeur,* as Aubert, in this instance. The printer of lithographs is *l'imprimeur* or *le lithographe,* the latter word being also a name for the artist of a lithograph. The print itself is *une lithographie.*

26 There is a biting lithograph by Raffet about the civil list in *La Caricature,* No. 11, 13 January 1831. Some authorities place the announcement of the royal budget in December 1830. If it were before 1 December 1830, it would give further and stronger meaning to Daumier's lithograph *Pauvres moutons* (D. 18) of that date.

27 *La Caricature,* No. 17, 24 February 1831; No. 21, 24 March 1831; and No. 22, 31 March 1831.

28 Ibid., No. 21, 24 March 1831.

29 Quoted in Jean Cherpin, *L'Homme Daumier,* Marseille, 1973, pp. 50–51.

30 Two previously considered lithographs may safely be removed from contention as possible Daumier prints: a) *Je dépose cela dans vos consciences* [I leave this to your consciences], probably of 1831, was attributed to Daumier by Hazard and Delteil, p. 58. In his later catalogue raisonné, Delteil relegated it to his Appendix as no. 28. His implication that it is not by Daumier is certainly correct. No other attribution is immediately apparent; and b) The unsigned lithograph, *L'âne chargé de reliques* [Donkey laden with holy relics], which appeared in *La Caricature,* No. 58, of 8 December 1831, was attributed to Daumier by Arsène Alexandre, p. 30 and p. 365. The suggestion was picked up by Howard P. Vincent, *Daumier and His World,* Evanston, Ill., 1968, p. 245, note 4, who hesitated to make a full commitment. In my opinion, the lithograph is definitely not by Daumier. A comparison of the small figures in the surrounding crowd with similar figures in *Gargantua,* of almost the same date, shows a completely different artistic method. Hazard and Delteil, p. 793, give it to Emile Wattier. Surely the old attribution can be laid to rest. N.B.: This lithograph should not be confused with a Daumier woodcut of the same title that appeared in 1834 (Delteil, Appendix, no. 8).

31 *La Caricature,* No. 26, 28 April 1831, and No. 32, 9 June 1831.

32 Ibid., No. 29, 19 May 1831.

33 Ibid., No. 30, 26 May 1831, which gives a full trial transcript.

34 Ibid., No. 29, 19 May 1831.

35 *Hommage à Honoré Daumier,* no. 7, p. 34.

36 Vincent, p. 24.

37 The common practice of hand coloring lithographs needs a separate study. The work was done in lithographers' shops by craftsmen who did only coloring. Colored prints were generally preferred by collectors at that time. The contrary holds true today, which has led to neglect of the subject.

38 Delteil, nos. 56, 156. It is somewhat more akin to the portrait in the group scene in *Le Charenton ministérielle* (D. 44).

39 There is no evidence to support a possible attribution of this print to Grandville, as Delteil suggests. The style is Daumier's in every detail. There is also a proof known to have come from Philipon's collection that is labeled as being by Daumier, see Hôtel Drouot auction catalogue, 7–8 December 1966, lot 63.

40 Delteil, no. 28. The comment was apparently copied from Escholier, 1923, p. 22. Balzer, p. 35, suggests that the demonstrations following the fall of Warsaw in September 1831 were the most likely inspiration for this print. Alexandre, p. 31, also singles it out for special attention.

41 Delteil, no. 28.

42 Philipon's lithograph appeared in *La Caricature,* No. 35, 30 June 1831. Illustrated in Balzer, pl. 17.

43 *La Caricature,* No. 55, 17 November 1831, which quotes Philipon's whole speech to the jury.

44 Ibid., No. 56, 24 November 1831. The print is illustrated in Balzer, pl. 16, and in Vincent, p. 19, among others. It was seized by the police, as noted in *La Caricature,* No. 60, 22 December 1831.

45 *La Caricature,* No. 55, 17 November 1831. Aubert and Delaporte were acquitted of the same charge.

46 Adhémar and Lethève, p. 450.

47 Hazard and Delteil, p. 53.

48 *La Caricature,* No. 59, 15 December 1831.

49 Delteil, no. 32.

50 It might be noted that two states of this print are now known: one before the name of the printer, *Lith. de Delaunois,* was added at the lower right, the second after the addition.

51 Balzer, p. 14.

52 Alexandre, p. 46.

53 Several sources also mention a pamphlet by the Viscount de Cormenin, an "open letter" published in early December 1831 that sarcastically attacked the "civil list" and its associated taxes. In fairness, it should be mentioned that the previous king, Charles X, enjoyed an annual royal appropriation of forty million francs.

54 Delteil, no. 34, describes a first-state proof inscribed *La Caricature (Journal)* and "On s'abonne chez Aubert," phrases that were reversed for the actual *Caricature* lithographs. The inscriptions were subsequently removed.

55 *La Caricature,* No. 61, 29 December 1831.

56 Ibid., No. 64, 19 January 1832.

57 Ibid., No. 66, 2 February 1832. The offending print was in No. 52, 26 October 1831.

58 Each issue of *La Caricature* was numbered consecutively from No. 1 through No. 251. In addition, each lithograph was assigned a plate number. Because there were usually two lithographs in each issue, the two numerical series are closely related. Double-size prints often received a double plate number.

59 This print, like all those that appeared in *La Caricature* proper, had the special inscription, *On s'abonne chez Aubert* [subscribe at Aubert's]. The point was that one could obtain *Caricature* lithographs only by subscribing to the journal for a minimum of three months. No examples of the prints were available at Aubert's except by subscription. It was a good method of gaining new subscribers, and the limitation seems to have been scrupulously observed throughout at least this early period of *La Caricature*.

60 Hazard and Delteil, p. 56.

61 At this point, Delteil departed from a strictly chronological numbering. He grouped the Aubert-published prints, nos. 35–39, before the *Caricature* ones, nos. 40 ff. Because they are presented here in the order of publication and copyright deposit dates, Delteil's numbers are not in sequence.

62 Vincent, p. 29.

63 Quoted in Delteil, no. 34, and *Hommage à Honoré Daumier*, p. 35.

64 *La Caricature*, No. 17, 24 February 1831; No. 55, 17 November 1831; and No. 66, 2 February 1832 (Philipon's speech only).

65 Ibid., No. 70, 1 March 1832.

66 Delteil, no. 42.

67 See Adhémar, Paris, 1954, pp. 15–17, 20–21, ill. opp. p. 23, for a detailed consideration of some of the caricatural influences on Daumier. See also idem, "Daumier et Boilly," *Arts et Livres de Provence*, 2, 1955, pp. 18–20.

68 Grandville's "*Te deum à l'autel*, 1ère planche," in *La Caricature*, No. 53, 5 November 1831, the third face from the right.

69 See Jeanne L. Wasserman, *Daumier Sculpture: A Critical and Comparative Study*, Greenwich, Conn., 1969, an invaluable catalogue raisonné.

70 The print bears the inscription "*chez Aubert, E^eur du J^al la caricature, galerie véro dodat*," which may be a simple error, or may indicate that the print was first intended for sale at Aubert's, and that Philipon made a last-minute decision to include it in *La Caricature*.

71 *La Caricature*, No. 72, 15 March 1832.

72 Ibid., No. 13, 27 January 1831.

73 Wasserman, p. 106, has biographical information about Lameth, as well as commentary on the use of the sculpted model.

74 In contrast to *Masques de 1831*, this print has the inscription reserved for *La Caricature*: "*On s'abonne chez Aubert. . . .*" It did not, in fact, appear in the journal, but only at Aubert's.

75 Alexandre, p. 361.

76 *La Caricature*, No. 82, 24 May 1832.

77 These captions have been transcribed and the individuals identified by Hazard and Delteil, pp. 66–67.

78 *La Caricature*, No. 86, 28 June 1832.

79 Wasserman, p. 69.

80 Ibid., p. 158.

81 It seems odd that copyright deposits should have been made on the national holiday, but that is how the date is recorded (Delteil, no. 37).

82 This and several other Daumier prints done for Aubert have a series title *Caricatures politiques*. Such series were commonly instituted by print publishers, purely as a means of encouraging sales. It is well known that collectors like to buy things in series. If one sees a "No. 31" and a "No. 33," one becomes curious about "No. 32." Prints in such series were often by different artists and had no thematic connection other than general political subject matter. Another such series from Aubert in which Daumier's prints appeared was *Séries poli*. The abbreviation lends itself to a double meaning, either "political series" or "polite series." See, for instance, Delteil 27.

83 There is a brief description of this print in *La Caricature*, No. 89, 19 July 1832.

84 Ibid., No. 88, 12 July 1832.

85 Ibid., No. 92, 9 August 1832. An earlier issue, No. 43, 25 August 1831, stated that 28,847 crosses had been distributed to that date.

86 Ibid., No. 89, 19 July 1832.

87 Ibid., No. 90, 26 July 1832.

88 Delteil, nos. 131–135. Bechtel illustrates and discusses all twenty-four prints. *La Caricature* arranged that subscribers both to the journal and the association would receive their monthly lithograph along with *La Caricature*, which explains why most of the association prints are found with a centerfold. They are folded to fit inside the journal.

89 *La Caricature*, No. 91, 2 August 1832.

90 Wasserman, pp. 44–47.

91 Maurice Gobin, *Daumier Sculpture*, Geneva, 1952, p. 226, reproduces, with an exasperating lack of documentation, a fragment of an unpublished lithographic portrait of d'Argout. It might be by Daumier, but there is no way of telling without seeing the whole print.

92 The man in the middle has usually been identified, notably by Delteil, as Gisquet, the Paris prefect of police. The error traces back to Champfleury (pseud. of Jules Fleury), *Histoire de la Caricature moderne*, Paris [1865], p. 68. It was finally corrected in *Hommage à Honoré Daumier*, 1968, p. 35. The resemblance to d'Argout, as seen in the preceding print, is too striking to be ignored. Also *La Caricature*, No. 94, 23 August 1832, refers to "two ministers and an attorney general"; Gisquet was not a minister of state.

93 These have been transcribed and the individuals identified by Hazard and Delteil, p. 67.

94 *La Caricature*, No. 95, 30 August 1832.

95 Vincent, p. 30, p. 245, note 8, discovered the arrest order, dated 27 August 1832, in the Archives de la Seine. Bernard Lehmann, "Daumier Père and Daumier Fils," *Gazette des Beaux-Arts*, 27, May 1945, pp. 309–310, had earlier found the jail-book entry of 31 August 1832, in the same archive.

96 Even the lithographs done by Charles Ramelet after Daumier's prison drawings did not start to appear until about the time of his release. The first of them was published in *Le Charivari*, 14 January 1833. See Delteil, Appendix, no. 29 ff.

97 Alexandre, p. 52.

Peter Morse, formerly associate curator of graphic arts at the Smithsonian Institution, is research associate at the Honolulu Academy of Arts. He is the author of *John Sloan's Prints*, New Haven, 1969, *Jean Charlot's Prints: A Catalogue Raisonné*, Honolulu, 1976, and numerous articles on prints and printmaking.

Fig. 1. *Célèbrrrrrre Jury de Peinture . . .* (Delteil 557).

Jean Charlot

Daumier's Graphic Compositions

As had Rembrandt before him, Honoré Daumier at times graphically expressed his own ideas about those who have ideas about art. With Dutch bluntness, Rembrandt feigned agreement with contemporary critics who accused him of neglecting ideal beauty by sketching himself pants down, defecating over a canvas laid flat on the floor. Daumier, with French finesse, felt equally free to analyze what motley ideals, if any, moved the bigwigs who juried the official art event, the annual Salon. In a lithograph dating from the mid-nineteenth century (Fig.1), he describes the setting, a storage room where the pictures to be judged are propped haphazardly against the walls. Most jurors rudely turn their backs on the paintings, one yawns frantically. Obviously these vote nay. Three others, however, show a more open mind in that each assays the display against the touchstone of his personal ideal. One, dreaming of an art hitched high to a star, peers through a telescope angled toward infinity, thus missing the canvases heaped at his feet. A second, swayed by audiophone reveries, plays his violin to check if color and brushstrokes are in key with his melody. A third bends low. Armed with a carpenter's compass he traces in the dust of the storeroom floor segments of circles that intersect triangles and rectangles. The year is 1840. Is this man a prophet, envisioning things to come, cubism or geometric abstractions? Or is he old-fashioned enough to sigh for the polyhedral projections that engrossed a Luca Pacioli?

Célèbrrrrrre Jury de Peinture, states the caption, as if to reassure us that these eccentric jurors are no more than puppets, created to raise a chuckle. Nevertheless, may one learn from this scene something of the aesthetic creed of Daumier the artist?

His crayon damns the jurors who turn their backs on what they are sworn to appraise. It softens its harshness as regards the well-meaning trio that at least is in earnest. High ideals (the astronomer), harmonious rhythms (the violinist), cool logic (the geometrician) are indeed ingredients found in Daumier's art. It was hitched to a star, a political one at its core, this Republic for which he pined and fought through the reigns of two kings and an emperor. As to music, his complex orchestration of chiaroscuros prompted Théophile Gautier to remark, "There is something of Michelangelo in that fellow." This paper, somehow, means to focus on a third and less publicized ingredient of Daumier's style: the devising of ordered compositions that the third juror, compass in hand, may for our purpose personify.

Geometry and story-telling

Fifteenth-century master painters, exacting craftsmen though they were, reached out for the realm of *cosa mentale*, that elusive entity that young Leonardo rated far above craft. Paolo Uccello wrestled a lifetime with perspective problems. First he would draft a linear rendering of a cube, check and recheck its geometrical accuracy, and only then add what accessories transformed it into a room, set as a stage for the display of some dramatic episode. In a panel of the famed Urbino predella, while the guilty one cowers behind a closed door, the soldiery wrathfully rams it into splinters. Is such a display of force truly necessary to demolish a feat of projective geometry?

Contrariwise, Daumier's images of a three-

(Photographs kindly supplied by the author.)

55

Fig. 2. *Madame déménage!* (Delteil 3590).

naires, barbarians, the victors and the dead, bunched as grapes on a stem. Daumier kept at home a cast from Trajan's column. Haphazard though it was, this classical training made him aware of the basic grandeur of geometric solids. Cylinders, pyramids, spheres buttress some of his graphics, translated, as may be inferred, into his peculiar city slang.

Cylinders can be news. *Madame déménage* (Fig. 2), a nightmarish Death astride the boiler of her locomotive, speeds ahead full steam. More prosaically, *Société catholique du Baptême organisée pour le salut des buveurs parisiens . . .* (Fig. 3), workers unloading casks of wine, rolling and piling them on the quays of Bercy, the barrels not unlike fragmented columns, their flaring profiles aping the Greek module. This straightforward rendering contrasts with a bizarre follow-up, *C'est un peu dur d'être obligé . . .* (Fig. 4). In mid-century, many Parisians were rendered homeless by the razing of whole quarters of the city, brought about by Baron Haussmann's inflexible will to make place for the Grands Boulevards. Putting the casks seen on the quays of Bercy to surrealistic uses, Daumier depicts folks who attempt to live in barrels, deploring the fact they are no Diogenes.

M. Prud'homme se passant la fantaisie . . . (Fig. 5) adapts the cone, or rather here the pyramid, to the headlines of the day. *Turcos*, fez-coiffed, dark-skinned Algerian troops on their way to the Crimea, encamped on the Champs de Mars, an exotic sight that drew Parisian idlers.

The sphere is recurringly newsworthy. Balloons make news. *Nadar élevant le Photographie à la hauteur de l'Art* (D. 3248; see Stein, Fig. 15) hails the birth of aerial photography. *L'Equilibre européen* (Fig. 6) features another kind of sphere, our planet, precariously balanced on the points of bayonets. In 1856, fashions changed radically. Crinolines, ballooning over metal hoops, filled promenades with their domical silky shapes. *Nouvelles modes du demi-monde . . .* (Fig. 7), drawing a parallel with the hoop-petticoats of the preceding century, is fairly realistic reporting. Published less than a week later, *Manière d'utiliser les jupons . . .* (Fig. 8) creates a phantasmagory wherein pretty messengers of the new fashion parachute to earth from some empyrean heights!

One rectangular solid, basic to Daumier's compositions, was not entirely of his free choice. Its six facets echoed in depth the rectangle that the format of the illustrated weeklies imposed. We shall refer to it loosely as a cube. On this one motif Daumier played endless variations, but, before analyzing this limited pictorial space in which his personages most often move and breathe, let us attempt to define his personal conception of the picture plane.

dimensional world started from direct observation. He did not handle compass and ruler but neither did he draw from the model before attacking the lithographic stone. He puzzled at the doings of his artist friends, Charles-François Daubigny among them. Like hunters they left home at daybreak in quest of a motif, shod with high boots, a heavy back pack, holding an alpenstock *en lieu* of a gun. The quarry sought was a landscape worthy of their brush, Barbizon oaks preferred. Daumier's hunting grounds spanned the whole city, including unusual haunts that Emile Zola would later rediscover and describe in *Le Ventre de Paris*. Daumier befriended all workers, market strong men, stevedores, butchers, and bakers, but on his strolls would leave at home, if ever he owned one, his sketchbook. His true subject was life's flow and he did not care to freeze, even for a moment, its vital rhythms.

He also treasured museum memories, Alexandre Lenoir's Musée des Monuments Français and visits to the Louvre, lingering in sculpture halls. Over Greek marbles smooth as soap he rated Roman bronze bas-reliefs molded by anonymous jobbers, Caesars, horses, legion-

57

Fig. 3. *Société catholique du Baptème organisée pour le salut des buveurs parisiens . . .* (Delteil 1016).

Fig. 4. *C'est un peu dur d'être obligé de se loger dans un tonneau . . .* (Delteil 2575).

Fig. 5. M. *Prud'homme se passant la fantaisie . . .* (Delteil 3194).   **Fig. 6.** *L'Equilibre européen* (Delteil 3540).

Artisanal concept of the picture plane

Daumier was not a bookish man, and little inclined to ponder Euclidean absolutes. It was rather his heightened visual experience that taught him wordlessly how to build a geometric underpinning for his compositions. It is therefore pertinent to survey the milieu in which his lithographs were created.

Among his working companions at the publisher's shop, he identified readily with the manual worker, the printer, an apron at his waist, cockily coiffed with the badge of his trade, a paper cap of folded proof sheets. Daumier lovingly depicts him at work, manning the handle of a Stanhope press (D-71), or boldly defying kings, sleeves rolled up, ready at a dare to erect street barricades (D-133). Daumier felt less at ease with another group of equally dedicated coworkers, the white-collar wits whose tool was the pen. He rarely bothered with the word for word of his captions, and came to feel a strong dislike for the famed set of *One Hundred and One Robert Macaires*, because of its overflowing and involuted dialogues, created with special care and pride by Charles Philipon.

Daumier nursed no illusion as to the fate of his weekly cartoons, barred from the haughty seclusion of connoisseurs' portfolios. For the subscriber to *Le Caricature* or *Le Charivari*, his cartoons were little more than vignettes, a visual rest between text pages, to be flipped out of sight at will. The reader thought of them as drawn on paper but Daumier knew better. Four thousand times throughout his lifetime he sat or stood facing a block of stone quarried out of the Bavarian site whence came the stones that drove Aloys Senefelder to invent lithography.

As a practicing lithographer, I can testify that to handle stones, grain stones, and draw on them makes one familiar with each, its weight, its color, hardness, and idiosyncracies. This means more than an artisanal detail, and throws a sidelight on the oft-quoted pairing of Daumier with Michelangelo. The Italian loved stones for themselves, collecting choice Carrara blocks that he piled on papal plazas. As to Daumier, he lived his working hours among stones. At the start of each day's chore, propping one up, he faced a small architecture, a rectangular solid. Even though his task was to maculate its surface with crayon, Daumier could hardly escape the stone's solid assertion of self.

The image of the propped-up lithographic stone, mirrored day after working day on his retina, was fated to surface in his work, slightly camouflaged to play its part in a story. *Le Peuple Souverain* (Fig. 9), despite a hardly convincing superstructure and a hand-lettered assertion that this monolith is a ballot box, is stone; its

Manière d'utiliser les jupons nouvellement mis à la mode.

Fig. 8. *Manière d'utiliser les jupons nouvellement mis à la mode* (Delteil 2759).

shape, its thickness, its hardness, that of the lithographic stone.

Tu resteras dehors . . . (Fig. 10), the rotting imperial eagle crucified onto the Book of History; does it deal as stated with a book, symbolic though it be, or, unacknowledged even by Daumier, is it not rather a transmogrified image of the very stone he was facing when he drew this masterpiece?

Theoreticians, as they refer to the picture plane, conceive of it as an insubstantial entity. In a woodcut illustrating his *Treatise of Measurements*, published in 1525, Albrecht Dürer depicts a Rube Goldberg sort of machine. A hook with a string attached acts as a mechanical eye gathering to itself a cone of optical lines. An assistant, keeping the string taut, contacts with it a series of points on the surface of the model, in this example a lute. Somewhere on its course between hook and lute, the string passes within an empty frame. For each motion the master of the shop—artist, mathematician, or both—measures the distance from the string to the inner edges of the frame. Point after point is thus accurately reported on a gessoed panel and

LE PEUPLE SOUVERAIN

Fig. 9. *Le Peuple Souverain* (Delteil 3928).

a line threaded through the points. The result is a mechanical draft of the model, a linear photograph. Thus understood, the picture plane is literally a nothingness, a thin slice of air that only the solid frame marks as distinct from the air we breathe.

Artisanal common sense taught Daumier an opposite truth. As stated, his picture plane is stone, indeed hard to mistake for air. *Bas-relief en pain d' èpices* . . . (Fig. 11) quizzically illustrates the fact, transmuting stone into gingerbread, but it yet retains the grayness and the grain of the prepared surface, and borrows the stone's beveled edge, distinct from the ruled lines that routinely frame most of Daumier's published cartoons.

One of the last lithographs that Daumier ever drew features even more emphatically the solidity of the picture plane. *Ce que d'aucuns appellent un progrès* (Fig. 12) erects a vertical wall of planking that represents a pillory. For the moment untenanted, its left half exhibits holes for the head, hands, and feet of a culprit. Tenanted, the right half imprisons the Press, a woman coiffed with the telltale cap of folded news sheet, a pen in hand. Her head, hands, and feet protrude through the holes. So integrated with the picture plane are the planks of the pillory that head, hands, and feet visually jut forward, ahead of the page.

Progressive approach to depth

Lithography as his major graphic medium was not for Daumier a free choice. Through most of his lifetime it remained the cheapest and speediest way of multiplying an image and thus, for his budget-minded publishers, a must. That the craft induced in Daumier specific attitudes does not imply that his wish was to revolutionize or renovate. As skillfully as the best among his contemporaries, he knew how to conjure volume, space, depth, motion. Something, however, remains of his lithographer's scruples that stamp his solutions as distinctive. Even where depth is explicitly involved he reserves part of the image area to act as *repoussoir*, an opaque plane often left bare. Parallel to the picture plane, it is a vestigial reminder of the solid stone surface.

T'as tort de vouloir afficher cette grande annonce . . . (Fig. 13) is an extreme example in that this opaque plane, in this case a street wall,

« Tu resteras dehors et cloué sur la porte!... »

Fig. 10. *Tu resteras dehors et cloué sur la porte!* . . . (Delteil 3853).

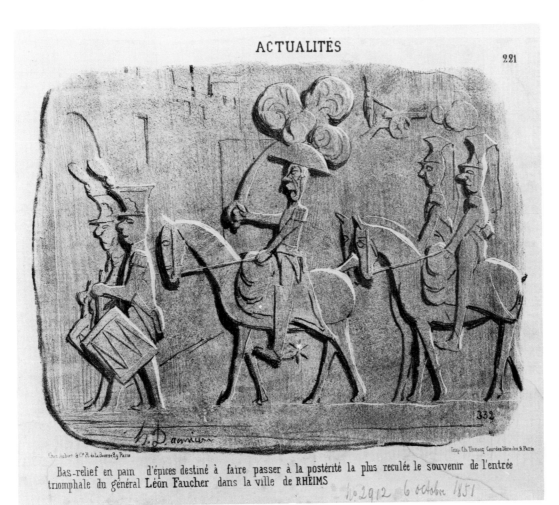

Fig. 11. *Bas-relief en pain d'épices destiné à faire passer . . .* (Delteil 2155).

Fig. 12. *Ce que d'aucuns appellent un progrès* (Delteil 3879).

Fig. 13. *T'as tort de voulour afficher cette grande annonce dans de mois-ci . . .* (Delteil 1270).

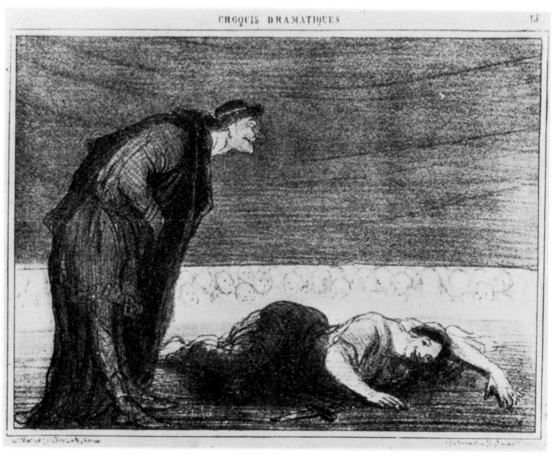

Fig. 14. *La Princesse—Voyons, être féroce, finis-en donc vite . . .* (Delteil 2909).

Fig. 15. *Une Reine se préparant à une grande tirade* (Delteil 2897).

spreads over the total area of the picture. The diagonal device of a raised ladder casting its shadow on the wall alerts the eye to the fact that between it and us lies a pocket of space. The wall is realistically plastered with posters, or rather broadsides—the pictorial poster being not yet current. Recent advertisements overlap dilapidated ones. The newest is just now being slapped plumb over the papered wall by a bill sticker, his square brush dripping paste. It proclaims how Chateaubriand's *Memoirs* start in serial form in a daily, *La Presse*. A few passersby stop and stare. Strictly parallel to the picture plane, the wall recedes in space ever so slightly, opening a corridor of space wide enough for Daumier's personages to move and breathe in.

In the next example, this opaque area opens thriftily to reveal a horizontal glimpse of deep space. *La Princesse—Voyons, être féroce, finis-en* . . . (Fig. 14) deals with the world of the theater. It locates the viewer upstage while a classical tragedy comes to its close. The togaed Roman has uttered the last syllables of a lengthy tirade. The heroine lies at his feet, presumably stabbed

to death. The stage lights have just been darkened, the curtain comes down. To "snap" the scene, Daumier chose the split second before it reaches the floor in its fall. Through the narrow strip still left gaping, we get a panoramic glimpse of the auditorium where lights are already blazing. Still seated, stunned by the traumatic ending, the audience will next burst into applause. The curtain, plainly rectangular, stops the eye as efficiently as did the street wall.

Une Reine se préparant à une grande tirade (Fig. 15) distributes equably the two opposites, open space and space walled out of sight. Viewed from the wings, the classical drama is caught in mid-course. The right half of the lithograph pictures the lighted part of the stage, a Roman orator strutting and orating, the spectators tiered vertically from pit to ceiling drinking in his eloquence.

Bathed in darkness, the left half hides from view the Queen. Prudently, she blows her nose to the full before crossing into public view and in her turn declaim! Here Daumier divides light from darkness, shallow space from deep

64

Fig. 16. *Des Parisiens dans l'attente du plaisir . . .* (Delteil 2652).

Fig. 17. *Nouvelle suspension aérienne* (Delteil 3552).

Fig. 18. *Bouderie conjugale* (Delteil 1561).

space, by the ragged edge of a stage flat. It stands in total contrast to the preceding device, a stage curtain as plain as a Euclidean figure.

When this device of an opaque area is omitted, Daumier nevertheless guides the eye back to the picture plane. *Des Parisiens dans l'attente du plaisir* (Fig. 16) shows patient citizens queuing outside a theater, expressively displaying frustration, hope, boredom, impatience, resignation. They are visually caged inside a stark combination of verticals and horizontals as impressively detached from human passions as an abstract by Piet Mondrian.

Even in scenes that deal with infinity, Daumier manages some linear device that ties in with the surface of the page. *Nouvelle suspension aérienne* (Fig. 17) represents Dame Europe lying magically relaxed on thin air, her elbow resting comfortably on the point of a bayonet. The right angle thus achieved is a forceful reminder of the rectangular format.

Exceptions strengthen the rule. *Bouderie conjugale* (Fig. 18) is one of the few compositions based in toto on unlimited space. To compare it with the previous examples should clarify the point.

Punch and Judy geometry

The Paris of Napoleon III, despite the boulevards abuilding, was, or so it seems in retrospect, still rustic. A relaxed walk through the Champs-Elysées bathed the Parisian in nature's lushness. On low benches lined under the chestnut trees moppets sat with their nurses, on occasion joined by Daumier himself. All watched delighted a Guignol play, the French Punch and Judy show. The theater itself was a portable affair, hardly more than a box, high enough and deep enough to hide from view the puppeteer and to store his stock of actors, sets, and accessories, the major one a bludgeon used for bastinadoes. *Marionnettes politiques* (Fig. 19), Monsieur Adolphe Thiers manipulating subservient congressmen, helps us visualize the layout from inside the puppeteer's stall.

What the audience saw was sheer magic. *Les principaux personnages de la Comédie . . .* (Fig. 20) presents a spectator's view of the stage, its uprights upholding a curved pediment, folksy version of a rococo gone to seed. Seen in full light against the shady depth, three marionettes, the royalist, the Bonapartist, and a cleric,

ACTUALITES.

Marionnettes politiques.

Fig. 19. *Marionnettes politiques* (Delteil 2003).

Fig. 20. *Les principaux personnages de la Comédie . . .* (Delteil 2156).

Fig. 21. *Le nouveau Polichinelle Napolitain* (Delteil 2636).

Commençant à rendre justice aux blanches.

Fig. 22 *Commençant à rendre justice aux blanches* (Delteil 3151).

do their thing. Enough is represented of the facade of the theater to identify it with the picture plane.

Le nouveau Polichinelle Napolitain (Fig. 21), identically composed, counterbalances the depth of the stage by a bold device previously met in dramatic context in *Ce que d'aucuns appellent un progrès* (Fig. 12). Here a heap of mock corpses, bastionadoed to death, overhang, heads bashed and arms limp, casting realistic shadows over the planks of the facade, thus occupying a space set ahead of the picture plane.

Daumier may well have failed to draw a strict demarcation between the behavior of puppets and that of humans. *Commençant à rendre justice aux blanches* (Fig. 22) marks a transition. The setting is that of a Guignol play, modified from a frontal to a three-quarter view to allow for a bit of landscape, a park where beauteous females promenade. Faustin Elie Soulouque, the exiled emperor of Haiti, ogles them from high. His house looks suspiciously like a Guignol box; the window he leans through could be its stage. The texture of the face of the august exile, a black, is treated as whittled wood rather than

Fig. 23. *Ménage modèle—depuis trente ans, ils cultivent la vertu . . .* (Delteil 1482).

L'EXPOSITION UNIVERSELLE.

Fig. 24. *Venant de donner le dernier coup de Pinceau* . . . (Delteil 2663).

human flesh. Soulouque holds his telescope like a bludgeon, the favorite prop of Polichinelle.

Ménage modèle . . . (Fig. 23) returns to the orthodox frontal view. Fully human, a husband and wife dawdle contentedly at their window, basking in the sunlight. Behind them one glimpses a shady interior. Though camouflaged with flower pots and vines, the essentials of the Guignol scheme are hardly modified.

That Daumier's approach to descriptive geometry was thus apparently casual, amused even, may prove deceptive. He confronts its problems with a oneness of purpose equal to that of fifteenth-century geometricians, men little inclined to watch Punch and Judy shows.

Story-telling as a means of composition

It would be misleading to present Daumier's geometrical leanings as a thought-out logical progession. Rather they parallel the happenings of a séance, wherein the ghostly visitor, often dimly perceived, materializes to the full on rare occasions.

Fig. 25. *Effet de lunes* (Delteil 648).

A key to Daumier's optical alphabet remains the rectangle, which in turn begets the cube. It was no brain child, however, but a rectangle his own eyes did see. While he worked, it was the surface of a stone maculate with crayon. Published, it translated into a sheet of paper smeared with ink. Between what his eye saw and what his hand drew, these sights suffered sea changes. Rectangles invade sundry themes, most obviously those related to painters and their paintings. The stretcher bars' mitred square, the sculptured and gaudily gilded frames inspired Daumier more often than the brushwork, portraits, still lifes, or landscapes.

The tales he tells have simple plots. Pridefully the artist brings his pictures to the official Salon (D. 2664). Mournfully he returns home, his rejected masterpieces laid on a stretcher (D. 2665). The Salon opens, disclosing pictures hung row upon row as sardines laid in a can (D. 3294). The famous art critic whisks through, notebook in hand, painters curtseying in his path (D. 3448). Thus the themes told in human terms. Optically, a single title fits them all, "In Praise of the Rectangle."

Venant de donner le dernier coup de pinceau . . . (Fig. 24) illustrates the point. Having brushed in his last stroke and elated at the result, the painter improvises a self-congratulatory jig. The ill-kept studio is a visual encyclopedia of rectangles, of all sizes and seen in all perspectives, versos and rectos, plumb and off-plumb, vying with the dancer in angularities.

Weary of perspective lines that smack of the blackboard, Daumier treads cautiously into regulated depth. Suggestions, rather than descriptions, abound. *Effet de lunes* (Fig. 25) features a window, a French window, of course, both its casements open at an angle. Hinged together, the three rectangular planes create a recess that accommodates a couple gazing at the moon. True, the stark trio of rectangles opens on a vista of the night sky. Disregard the view, or rather minimize it as one would a painted backdrop, a favorite accessory of nineteenth-century portrait photographers. Concentrate instead on the orderly presentation of measured space in the foreground, though it is, as Daumier wished it, willfully understated.

A Clichy . . . (Fig. 26) uses an identical setting to express a more astringent mood. Two inmates of a jail for debtors face an open window. The serried verticals of its prison bars force their eyes and ours back to the foreground with its Spartan spatial scheme.

Un Français peint par lui-même (Fig. 27) is more tightly articulated. Canvas and easel are

Fig. 26. *A Clichy.—Dire que dans quelques semaines . . .* (Delteil 3423).

Fig. 27. *Un Français peint par lui-même* (Delteil 1722).

Fig. 28. *Voila une bonne hauteur pour mettre mon baromètre . . .* (Delteil 1622).

guage with abstract geometry. One follows the index finger of John the Baptist to its goal, Christ. Was Titian unaware of the casually self-centered gesture of his reclining Venuses? Here Daumier's painter, engrossed in his work—if not Gustave Courbet himself, one of his followers—performs a more complex task than painting. Both his hands and his ego are tied to the job, but his head and eyes, pivoting from mirror to canvas and from canvas to mirror, involve the viewer in their alternate scanning. Were it not for this device, both psychological and mechanical, the dynamics of the scene would come to a stop.

The cube

It is easier to express depth than lack of depth. The human eye, highly trained by everyday experience, sees depth even when the painter did not so wish. A rectangle within a rectangle—any one of Josef Albers' *In Praise of the Square*—may be interpreted in depth (Drwg. A). To will depth, to emphasize depth, add webs of lines converging toward infinity, cut short at their junction by the inner rectangle (Drwg. B). Translating them as beams on a ceiling and pavement on a floor, Uccello, in one of the panels of the Urbino predella, has left us a cool masterpiece, wherein linear purity outweighs human drama (Drwg. C).

To describe a cubic space, Daumier favors this frontal view. Its surface echoes the format of the page. Read in three dimensions, Parisians, who live inside cubes, enrich the familiar sight with their own memories. *Voila une bonne hauteur pour mettre mon baromètre . . .* (Fig. 28) features a cubic space, set for the nonce in linear perspective. To add zest to this geometric draft, Daumier adds a pinch of psychology. Could we doubt the cube is meant as a room when we watch the caged couple measuring its width and its height? The husband promenades a tape measure against its walls. His spouse checks the verticals by tapping the tip of her umbrella against the ceiling.

In *Il faut me trouver là-dedans trois pièces . . .* (Fig. 29), Daumier, with a few swift strokes, sets in orthodox perspective the naked inside of

parallel to the picture plane. Set at a right angle to it, the mirror activates perspective lines that guide the eye from surface to depth. The corner of the studio is an enlarged echo of the angular setup seen in the foreground.

Both cubist and abstractionist delved in our century into the relation of planes. Despising the anecdotal, both deemed story-telling an unforgivable faux pas. For Daumier, naive if you wish, the plot, the visual pun even, were never shunned but sought. Granted that his livelihood depended on it, nevertheless it was no concession on his part. Memories of the museum taught him how to interlace body lan-

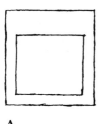

A

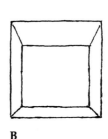

B

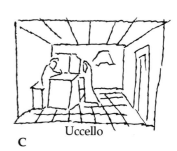

Uccello

C

Fig. 29. *Il faut me trouver là-dedans trois pièces . . .* (Delteil 2838).

Fig. 30. *Train de plaisir de Paris à St-Germain:— Wagon de deuxième classe* (Delteil 2283).

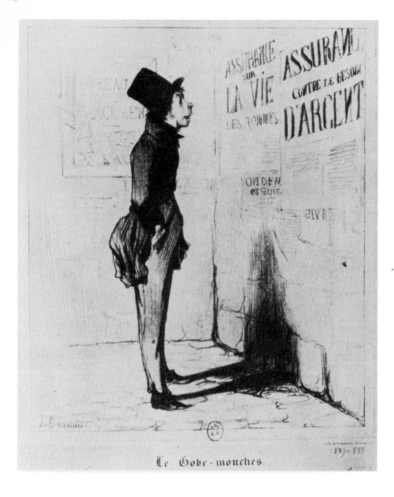

Le Gobe-mouches.

EMOTIONS PARISIENNES.

Fig. 31. *Le Gobe-mouches. L'origine de cet animal se perd . . .* (Delteil 527).

a cube. A single window transforms it into a room. A greedy landlord, bent on remodeling this vacuum into a rentable apartment, confers with his mason. To illustrate the landlord's stinginess, Daumier lowers the ceiling until the heads of both personages butt hard against it. A visual joke, granted, but also a serious means of emphasizing cubic depth. Added to the shadows cast on the floor, those diagonally cast on the ceiling intensify with their chiaroscuro the reality of the cubic space at which the linear draft merely hinted.

In mid-century, to cubic rooms were added, thanks to a newfangled invention, the railway, cubes on wheels. Daumier sharpened his wit watching a handful of people, strangers to each other, crowd like cattle in this novel kind of box. *Train de plaisir de Paris à S^{L}Germain . . .* (Fig. 30) traps the travelers in the perspective web of a passenger car, the austere grayness of the bare interior contrasting with the lighted outer space and the lightning speed of the rushing landscape glimpsed through the window.

Psychology as a visual means

Besides using as a working cog in his compositions patterns of human behavior, Daumier handles another means equally out of bounds for the geometrician, chiaroscuro. Courbet, a contemporary, used it to make explicit the solidity of forms. Daumier favors it for another reason, as a worthwhile detour to bypass linear perspective. To differentiate shallow space from deep space he emphasizes contrasts between areas of light and dark far beyond any realistic purpose. In *Il faut me trouver là-dedans trois pièces* (Fig. 29) we saw how a room barely suggested by a few scribbled lines acquired substantial credibility once chiaroscuro came into play.

Le Gobe-mouches . . . (Fig. 31) illustrates that same point with primer-book clarity. The adolescent scanning street ads—could it be young Daumier at his first job, carrying documents from lawyers' desks to courtrooms?—would be planted in a near vacuum, were it not for the resolutely dominant cast shadow crawling on the pavement to break at a right angle as it climbs up the vertical wall, thus defining the locus of the scene.

When pressed for time, Daumier seldom hesitated to involve the viewer by presenting him

Fig. 32. *Ah bah! . . . Le locataire du premier, qui prend la taille de mon épouse! . . .* (Delteil 704).

Fig. 33. *L'Acteur . . . On voit bien qu'il fait chaud . . . trois spectateurs . . .* (Delteil 2826).

with a scent to follow. He banked on the fact that nineteenth-century Parisians were born, lived, and died in rooms, apartment buildings being to them what the hive is to the bee. The concierge, a more tyrannical figure than today's janitor, ruled the human hive. From his *loge,* a cubicle poised at the crossroads of all comings and goings, he missed little. What he did miss was more than made up by what he inferred while dusting stairs and corridors. Keyholes were his watchtowers.

Ah bah! . . . Le locataire du premier . . . (Fig. 32) is staged on the landing between a stairhead and an apartment door. A keyhole, technically a crayon dot, is the simple device that, besides implying unseen vistas, reaffirms the opacity, hence the reality, of the skimpily sketched architecture. As the concierge locks his eye to the keyhole so do we.

Gifted with a trained imagination, Daumier confidently leaves much, indeed at times most, to the viewer's imagination. His pictorial shorthand need not be commensurate with the complexity of an episode. *L'Acteur . . . On voit bien qu'il fait chaud . . .* (Fig. 33) brings us back to the theatrical world as seen from the wings. The curtain is down, the stage in darkness, the auditorium lit, the play not yet begun. Technically, Daumier covered the surface of the lithographic stone with a crayon halftone on which is sketched, black on gray, a pair of indistinct silhouettes, the director and an actress. Two white dots are scraped out of the halftone, peepholes through which the disheartened couple surveys a deserted auditorium.

Keyholes, peepholes, add interest to the vertical planes that limit the ever recurrent cubic space. At other times, Daumier wills us to focus on one of the horizontal planes, up or down, ceiling or floor. *Ah! ça Mais . . . arriverons-nous bientôt? . . .* (Fig. 34) rivets our attention to the floor. Improbably, yet assuredly, hugging the planking with its bewhiskered chin, there appears a human head, bespectacled, topped with a high hat. The conundrum is no sooner stated than solved, but, in that split instant, that sight has made us forget the normalcy of the setting. We are under the roof of an apartment house in the days when five floors and an attic counted as a skyscraper. A would-be renter, out of

Fig. 34. *Ah! ça Mais . . . arriverons-nous bientôt? . . .* (Delteil 1610).

Fig. 35. *Le Président de la diète ou le double Damoclès!* (Delteil 3507).

breath, apparently has switched in his climb from stairs to a ladder. At last his eyes are level with the mansarded garret. The concierge, for once, seems apologetic.

Le Président de la diète . . . (Fig. 35), a political cartoon whose subject would call for a learned historical footnote, concentrates our attention upward. A variant of the classical plight of Damocles, it shows the diplomat comfortably seated at a table, yet most uneasy, as two swords, lethally sharp, hang by threads over his head from the ceiling. At least this is what we think we see. Facts are otherwise. Daumier totally skips any representation of the ceiling, unless one accepts the routinely ruled horizontal line that tops the image as its schematic equivalent. Nevertheless, our preconception that this invisible ceiling supports the weight of two hanging swords gives it a solidity, hence a reality, that no crayon work, however detailed, could equal. As a successful device to focus our attention, this one ventures further into the minimal than even keyholes or peepholes. As drawing goes, this ceiling is less than a dot, it is literally nothing.

Cube begets cube

Uccello created a timeless image of a cube of air encased in an architecture (Drwg. C). Vittore Carpaccio, in his *Dream of Saint Ursula*, treats with equal clarity the theme of a cube set within a cube. Once a mural panel part of a decorative ensemble, Carpaccio's presentation is heavily caparisoned in Renaissance trappings. These should be visually bypassed the better to savor the essential simplicity of the composition. In a palatial hall stands a sumptuous bed, its rectangular canopy held high by four columnar bedposts. One would expect curtains to shield the sleeper, but the painter, keen on story-telling, wants us to know that, at that very moment, Saint Ursula lies in bed, lost in a prophetic dream. To that purpose, curtains are omitted, exposing her in virginal slumber as if she were a living relic encased in a crystal cube. Story-telling aside, the bed, its six rectangular planes punctiliously parallel to the walls, floor, and ceiling, stands as a cubic solid set amid a cube of space (Drwg. D).

The stage on which Daumier props his personages is limited in length, width, and depth, a box lying on its side, open toward the spectator. Only once have we seen this cube of space bare (Fig. 28). Each subject, as a rule, calls for a distinct backdrop and related accessories.

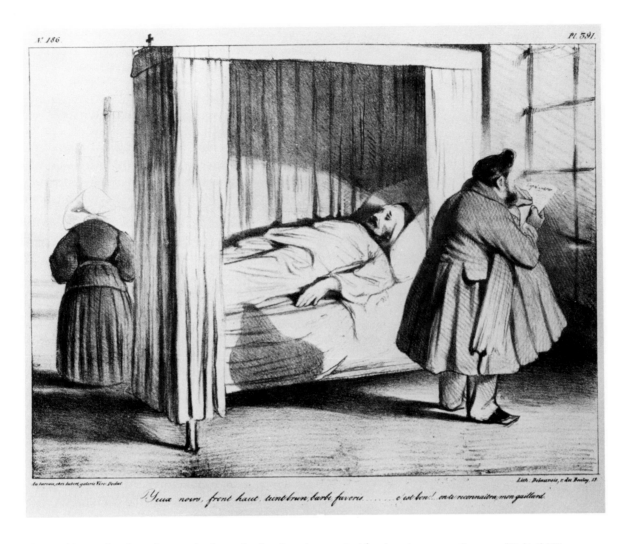

Fig. 36. *Yeux noirs, front haut, teint brun, barbe, favoris . . . c'est bon! on te reconnaîtra . . .* (Delteil 79).

Never visually verbose, Daumier refrains from strewing bric-a-brac as a realistic pretense. With a sense of geometrical fitness rooted in tradition, he pairs, whenever feasible, cubic solids with cubic space.

Since the fifteenth century, Carpaccio's bed had shrunk in size. The Paris bourgeois laid himself to sleep in a—by our standards—bed-size bed. By now, the canopy was a mere topknot that gathered the bed curtains into a tent shape. If Daumier is to be believed, in

Cappaccio

D

these rather shapeless recesses playlets were nightly performed, as disarmingly simple as those he watched, seated among moppets, at the Champs-Elysées.

Only in these most conservative of institutions, state hospitals run by nuns, had the antique types of bed, geometrically valid, survived. *Yeux noirs, front haut . . . on te reconnaîtra . . .* (Fig. 36) is a Carpaccio shorn of all superfluous ornaments. The hanging curtains, the bare walls, go straight to the marrow of the classical theme, a cubic solid set within a cubic space. Though soberly stated, the tale Daumier tells is not a whit less fabulous than the one Carpaccio told. We watch the king of the French, Louis-Philippe in person, jotting down the characteristics of a wounded opponent of his reign, the better to deliver him, on his return to health, to the mercies of his secret police.

A table is basically a cube. Old Masters knew it who significantly lengthened the tablecloth, thus rendering visible its four vertical planes. Often enough Daumier sketches the interior of drawing rooms and restaurants, furnished, naturally enough, with tables for his personages to

Les Etrangers à Paris.

3.

CE QU'ON APPÉLE **DINER** AU RESTAURANT.

Chez Aubert & C.ie Pl. de la Bourse, 29.   Imp. d'Aubert & C.ie

Fig. 37. *Ce qu'on appelle dîner au restaurant. Garçon! . . . voila une heure . . .* (Delteil 1274).

sit at and act their skit. The crayon stroke is cursive and casual, the characterizations witty. To insist that many of these genre scenes are, at the marrow, abstract would seem pedantic parlance. Yet it may be worth our while to probe along these lines. This we will do by comparing two drawings, similar and yet dissimilar, both having to do with tables.

For the *Charivari,* Daumier drew in the usual upright format *Ce qu'on appelle dîner au restaurant . . .* (Fig. 37). Table, tablecloth, a corner of the dining room, waiters and diners bespeak a sharply retentive memory seasoned with a dash of laughter.

Daumier worked at times for rival periodicals. The *Journal Amusant* called for a quite distinct format, an elongated rectangle laid horizontally. *Plus qu'un point!* . . . (Fig. 38) features a table, but it is now a billiard table seen lengthwise, its felt-covered top barely raised off the ground on stubby legs. The room too has suffered distortion. It is now a hall, low-ceilinged, so elongated that its lateral walls remain out of sight. Seated along the back wall and facing us, billiard lovers doze or watch the peripetes of the game. In the foreground two

LES JOUEURS DE BILLARD, — par H. Daumier.

— Plus qu'un point!... et une vraie paire de lunettes... pas de chance!!

Fig. 38. *Plus qu'un point!* . . . *et une vraie paire de lunettes* . . . (Delteil 3405).

LES GENS DE JUSTICE.

Fig. 39. *Oui, on veut dépouiller cet Orphelin . . .* (Delteil 1347).

players, cues in hand, face each other over the length of the board.

Pairing these two scenes proves instructive. When Daumier works for the *Charivari* verticals are features; horizontals for the *Journal Amusant*. Architecture, furniture, people even, all bend to the law that the distinctive formats state.

In the fifteenth century there was in Milan a monastic wall, gigantic when compared with the vignette of the *Journal Amusant*, but quite similar in its proportions. Contemporaries tell how Leonardo stood transfixed, gazing at it so often and so long that his patron, the prior, raged at his apparent laziness. To compare da Vinci's *Last Supper* with a Daumier cartoon may seem tactless only for those unacquainted with the genesis of true artistic creation. Both Daumier and Leonardo allowed the unusual proportions of each of the given areas to dictate its own solution, a frieze of personages half hid behind the horizontal of a table top running the full length of the low-lying rectangle. From then on, their paths separated. Da Vinci wrestled with God, Daumier donned his fool's cap.

In his teens a lawyer's jack-of-all-trades, jailed for the crime of lese majesty in his twen-

ties, young Daumier had had opportunity aplenty to measure the authority that a highback chair set behind a high bench confers on a judge, and how the formality of a boxed-in platform adds to the oratorical and physical gymnastics of both prosecutor and defender. Cubic in essence, this courtroom furniture was a good match for the basically cubic hall of law. These and similar adolescent musings were to bear rich fruits in later years. *Oui, on veut dépouiller cet Orphelin . . .* (Fig. 39) emphasizes the rigidity of the law by the use, exceptional for Daumier, of a ruler to draft with truly straight lines the carpentered paraphernalia.

Because interior scenes include furniture as one of the requirements of story-telling, the presence of beds, tables, or benches in pictures cannot be pointed to as a proof that Daumier juggles with cubes in a game of geometry. However, when he amalgamates dissimilar objects to conjure the image of a cubic solid, his goal, be it conscious or instinctive or both, is to echo in depth the rectangular format of the image. *Requiescat in Pace!* (Fig. 40) is a brutal image drawn in the 1870s when to failing eyesight was added a coarse semimechanical printing that did away with subtleties. In it Daumier the

POUVOIR TEMPOREL

AFFAIRES ETRANCÈRES

REQUIESCAT IN PACE!

Fig. 40. *Requiescat in Pace!* (Delteil 3871).

freethinker acclaims the annexation of the remaining Papal States to a recently unified Italy. In the foreground an embassy dispatch trunk, its lid open, its documents exposed in a rectangular pile, suggests steps ascending to what should be a throne. Instead, it leads us to a corpse totally hid under the folds of a shroud and stretched over a morgue slab. At its four corners stand four mortuary tapers, an incongruous parallel to Carpaccio's four columnar bedposts. High tapers and high bedposts alike delimit in space a cubic shaft. There is a difference, however. Carpaccio's bed is a glorified piece of furniture. Daumier's catafalque made of disparate elements projects in space the image of a cube only because he willed it so.

Hinged motions

A cube transformed into a room acquires accessories, hinged doors, hinged windows, mobile in that they can be shut or open. This fact may have suggested to Daumier a switch from static to dynamic manipulations of space. Some of them bring into play doors or windows, while others reach hesitantly toward a world of absolutes. Though varied, these dynamic devices

PROFESSEURS ET MOUTARDS.

Attends, attends ... j'te vas en donner moi du maitre d'école!...

Fig. 41. *Attends, attends, j'te vas en donner moi du maitre d'école!* (Delteil 1448).

Fig. 42. *Brigand de propriétaire . . . qui ne veut me faire faire des réparations . . .* (Delteil 1605).

may be basically diagrammed within a cube, one whose six sides are hinged, able to swing inward or outward in multiple combinations.

In *Attends, attends, j'te vas en donner moi du maître d'école!* (Fig. 41) a schoolmaster pushing open the door of the classroom surprises a small student seated at the master's desk, aping his mannerisms. An amusing skit, but, as happens so often with Daumier, intertwined with another, more detached, level of thought. As if to atone for the cluster of picturesque accessories and wealth of facial expressions, the door through which the schoolmaster enters is treated in shorthand, two ruled verticals, a nearly abstract rendering. That door functions in fact as one of the lateral facets of the cube, caught in inward motion.

Dynamic effects need not borrow, as does this one, from mobile accessories. A similar result is obtained by banking on the fact that the viewer anticipates the sight of an orthodox cube. Superposed on this preconceived image, the actual drawing, in essence cubic, will forcefully deviate in one essential part. *Brigand de propriétaire . . .* (Fig. 42) presents us with the inside of a room. As expected, its floor is horizontal, its walls vertical, but its ceiling slants perilously (Drwg. E). To the left, it has already

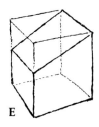

E

dropped halfway to the floor! A catastrophe, until we notice that this is an attic, tucked under the slope of a mansard roof, its ceiling built on an oblique. Nevertheless, that first instinctive reaction that "the sky is falling down" bathes in an atmosphere of geometric unease the very real plight of the tenant holding an open umbrella under the leaking roof, the gist of the story-telling.

To the hinged top of the cube dropping inward answers the rising up of its base to a diagonal position. In realistic terms, to the swing downward of the attic ceiling corresponds the slope upward of a flight of stairs. Daumier used

Fig. 43. *Grand escalier du Palais de justice. Vue de face* (Delteil 1372).

Fig. 44. *De ce côté-là vous voyez la tour Saint-Jacques la Boucherie!* . . . (Delteil 1603).

stairs to great effect in staging his playlets. In an apartment house, the staircase is his favorite meeting ground between landlord and tenants (D. 1613), and his favorite battleground between tenants and janitor (D. 1626). In public buildings stairs act monumental. A masterpiece, *Grand escalier du Palais de justice. Vue de face* (Fig. 43), seen in strictly frontal view, acquires majestic overtones. Displayed on a series of ascending horizontals, black-robed lawyers descend from the heights as did angels on Jacob's ladder. The abstract diagram is of utmost simplicity. Hinged to the lower edge of the vertical picture plane, the horizontal "floor" plane has revolved upward approximately thirty-five degrees. As was the case with the rain-drenched attic, the motion is illusive, the diagonal being set by the architect to instill in laymen contemplating the building a sense of awe at the majesty of the law.

De ce côté-là vous voyez la tour Saint-Jacques la Boucherie! . . . (Fig. 44) is based on the identical scheme displayed in three-quarter view. Hinged to the base of the picture plane, the "floor" plane of the cube has moved upward to a diagonal position (Drwg. F). However, while abstract and realistic elements dovetailed easily in the preceding example, here they part company. The hinged base of the cube has material-

ized into a roof! The skylight, raised even further than the slope of the major diagonal, acts as a small canopy over the severely restricted area where humans, or rather their disembodied heads, act and speak their skit. Thus freed from any role in the story-telling, the plain diagonal of the tiled roof acquires classical clarity.

Space represented (a) and space implied (b)

The dynamics involved in the preceding examples all occur within the confines of the basic cube. These inward motions emphasize the strictness of the cubic concept. At times, Daumier, wishing to escape from this spatial cage, will drop clues beyond these boundaries, either implied or explicit. In that sense, even a keyhole postulates unseen annexes to the primary cubic form. In *Effet de lunes* (Fig. 25) an open window becomes a triptych framing a limitless night sky.

Neither merely implied nor openly displayed, Daumier created, besides a series of forceful devices that leave us no choice but to mentally annex to the primary cube, an additional space that may be referred to as secondary. A first example introduces a rather abstract concept set within the everydayness of a bourgeois home.

Les Cabotins (Fig. 45) features a mirror before which a self-satisfied amateur applauds his own theatricals. But a mirror does not meekly reflect. It also holds magical properties, as Lewis Carroll's Alice found out when, boldly crossing over its threshold, she entered a room equal in every dimension to the one she had left behind. Frills aside, our primary cube—the room—theoretically duplicates itself on the other side of the mirror, thus doubling the span of the diagram. Correctly, Daumier situates the mirror at a right angle to the picture plane to be shared, recto and verso, by these Siamese twins, the primary cube and its reflected counterpart (Drwg. G).

Daumier is a master at enticing participation

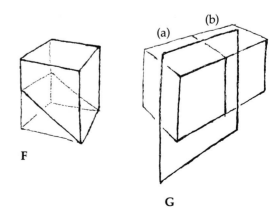

F

G

80

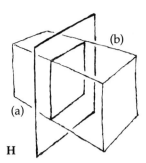

H

Fig. 45. *Les Cabotins* (Delteil 3949).

from the viewer. The janitor bent double at a keyhole tries our patience as we wait for our turn to see what he sees. More rarely, Daumier will catch our interest by a refusal to proffer clues, as in *On dit que les Parisiens . . .* (Fig. 46). Seen in strict frontal view, spectators crowd a theater pit, a sea of faces seemingly stretched to infinity. The pit is in darkness, only its first rows erratically lighted by the glow of the footlights. The play is on, all spectators are smiling. Thus, right ahead of the theater pit, if we are to believe what we see, the stage, wings, and greenroom raise their cubical architecture. In fact, I, the viewer, am on stage, my lines unrehearsed. Are they laughing with me or at me!

The motif of the twin cubes, first met in the preceding examples, is repeated here, but with a major variation. In *Les Cabotins* (Fig. 45), the mirror, set at a right angle to the picture plane, tied primary and secondary cubes into a diagram laid in pure profile. The mirror is replaced here (Fig. 46) by the picture plane, located where the stage curtain would fall. It links the crowded pit, receding in depth, with the stage and its adjuncts, jutting forward, enclosing within their ectoplasmic architecture the very locus that the viewer occupies. Thus, the device of the linked cubes is repeated, but turned around in a bold ninety-degree rotation (Drwg. H).

In 1840, King Louis-Philippe, in a move to refurbish his tarnished popularity, engineered the return of Napoleon's ashes from Saint Helena. Parisian crowds gawked as the monumental hearse draped in funereal violet made its slow progress under the Arc de Triomphe and down the Champs-Elysées. For permanent shelter an open crypt was planned, to be built in the Chapelle des Invalides where Louis XIV once had worshiped. Twelve sculptured Victories set in a circle would forever stand guard facing the sarcophagus of dark porphyry.

Before construction could begin, a crater-sized excavation was dug. Never a friend of kings or emperors, Daumier felt the moment propitious for a personal comment. *Le futur monument de Napoléon aux Invalides . . .* (Fig. 47) contrasts the classical dignity of the chapel with a disingenuous version of the work in course. Daumier often had raised a laugh by grafting giant heads on dwarf bodies, but here

Fig. 46. *On dit que les Parisiens sont difficiles à satisfaire . . .* (Delteil 3263).

81

Fig. 47. *Le futur monument de Napoléon aux Invalides. Voici l'entrée de la Chrilte . . .* (Delteil 981).

Fig. 48. *Examinant le nouveau plafond peint par Delacroix au Louvre* (Delteil 2228).

the comic effect is obtained by shrinking the majestic scale of the circular crypt to the size of a manhole, its lid gingerly raised by a peg-legged veteran acting as a guide. Bent double, visitors squint, attempting to pierce the darkness underfoot.

The chapel is the primary cube. The crypt is the secondary space, cylindrical in shape. Correcting Daumier's witty but unjust distortion of scale, the area shared by cylinder and cube is a circle inscribed into the square (Drwg. I). Both the diagrams of *Les Cabotins* and *On dit que les Parisiens* spread horizontally. Here the primary cube—the chapel—and the secondary cylinder—the crypt—are threaded on a vertical, the spectator's motion pointing downward.

Examinant le nouveau plafond peint par Delacroix , . . . (Fig. 48) takes us to the Louvre and the Galerie d'Apollon, named after the Sun God in fawning allusion to Louis XIV, Roi Soleil. The decoration of the gallery, begun in the mid-seventeenth century by Charles Le Brun, the king's own painter, had remained incomplete for two hundred years. Astonishingly, given the norms of officialdom, its completion was entrusted to Eugène Delacroix, most controversial among living artists. His painted ceiling was unveiled in 1852.

A ceiling has already played a major role in *Le Président de la diète . . .* (Fig. 35), but it was located within the limits of the picture area. Here we deal with a hall two hundred feet in length with a ceiling raised to a corresponding height. To keep the diagram in proportion, the vertical walls of the primary cube are prolonged upward, creating a rectangular shaft, its height twice that of the cube, topped by a horizontal "lid" that reaches the level of Delacroix' ceiling (Drwg. J).

While *Le futur monument de Napoléon . . .* (Fig. 47) funneled the interest of all participants, bent double, downward, here art critics and art lovers alike bend backward, all eyes focused heavenward.

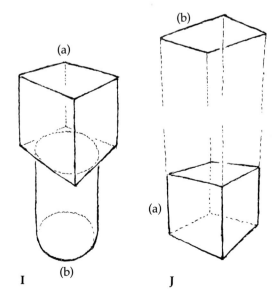

I   J

Of staircases

Daumier's graphic repertory borrowed its strength from sets and accessories that, for the Parisian of his day, acquired rich meaning through their undiluted everydayness. Early in our century the cubists were to do the same for their Paris, that was no longer Daumier's. In their still lifes, the pipe comes out of their pocket. From the package of tobacco they fill the pipe. On the match holder they scratch the match that lights the pipe. The newspaper, they peruse as they smoke.

Daumier's restricted visual vocabulary lacks even this mild bohemian flavor. Though he was not totally a bourgeois—the genius must have had its lodgings somehow inside him—he was as unmitigated an addict of the bourgeois as was Pieter Breughel, who was no peasant, of the peasant.

In Daumier's graphic work, staircase motifs loom large. Elevators were not in use, and climbing stairs was for the Parisian a daily must. The ascent started with a mild ceremonial gesture, the wiping of feet on the mat plus a short dialogue with the ever-watchful concierge. Then began a sort of safari for the homebound, the loss of plumb and the spiraling ascent. The staircases Daumier drew evoked in the nineteenth-century viewer reactions not merely visual. The palm of the hand gliding against the coolness of the bannister, the leg muscles reenacting their path upward and round about, the mild vertigo of a glance down the stairwell, the key noisily fumbling into the lock and at last, stability recovered, the change to slippers, the fireplace, the peace. While the self-contained interiors could be duplicated as stage sets, these spiral motions encircling a column of nothingness transcended theatrical make-believe. Daumier welcomed this dare to his creativeness. Let us compare two subjects, both related to the start of the ascent.

Ma femme est-elle à la maison? . . . (Fig. 49) presents a strict profile view of the stairs, their thrust upward roughly dividing the image in two triangular areas. The female concierge stands lower left, her proprietary stance underlined by a broom firmly grasped. The ascending lodger, half hid behind the oblique of the ramp, fits tightly at the upper right, his high hat pushing against the edge of the picture area.

L'Oubli de la consigne (Fig. 50) illustrates the identical scene caught full front. The stairs, represented by their superimposed uprights, fit along a vertical with just a trace of a spiraling torsion, then stop as they reach the horizontal landing. Seen from the back, the tenant takes

Fig. 49. *Ma femme est-elle à la maison? . . . Oui m'sieu . . .* (Delteil 1650).

Fig. 50. *L'Oubli de la consigne* (Delteil 1626).

the steps two by two, his off-balance emphasized by a violent foreshortening of the doubled-up left leg and the elongation of the right, the tip of its shoe still touching a lower tread. As before, the janitress is set plumb, stiff as her broom handle. Her index finger points to the mat at the foot of the stairs that the fellow, in his naiveté, had hoped to bypass.

These two identical episodes, one caught in strict profile and the other full front, could have been snapped simultaneously by two cameras set ninety degrees apart. At the start of his career, Daumier would model lumps of clay into the semblance of politicians that, from then on, remained at his mercy from whatever angle was needed. The procedure was not unusual. For his entry to the Salon of 1819, Géricault had had carpentered a reduced model of the raft of the *Medusa*, topping it with wax figures. In mid-career, however, Daumier, hurried and harried by deadlines, lacked leisure for such niceties, but the mental habit remained. Comparing both lithographs makes us realize with what conviction he grasped in depth the positioning of his personages within an architectural setting.

Checking the surface patterns exclusively, these two lithographs (Figs. 49, 50) seem totally unrelated. Disregarding the distinct sighting angles, however, a single diagram describes both. The lobby is the primary cube. The apartment implied at the level of the landing fills the secondary cube. The schema may be started with two equal planes bisecting each other in the shape of a Greek cross, their width that of a cube, their length twice their width. One half of the horizontal plane locates the ceiling of the lobby, the other half the level of the landing. The vertical plane similarly performs a split purpose. Its upper half stands for the frontage of the second-floor apartment, its lower half for the back wall of the lobby. Once completed, the diagram ties on an oblique the primary and secondary cubes, as dictated by the diagonal of the stairs (Drwg. K).

We have seen how effortlessly Daumier glided from factual reporting into a realm of utter fantasy. Barrels piled by lumpers on the quays of Bercy (Fig. 3) motivate a quizzical landscape strewn with barrels, each housing a disgruntled Diogenes (Fig. 4). The sketch of fashionables promenading at the Tuileries (Fig. 7) inspires the tumbling earthward of pretty parachutists clothed in the new fashion (Fig. 8). Daumier's staircase motifs, so realistically conceived that one could argue the use of three-dimensional

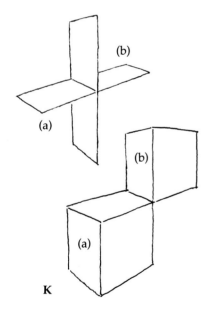

K

Fig. 51. *Les Parisiens à Cherbourg.—Eh! bien . . .*
nous ne sommes pas déjà trop mal . . . (Delteil 3062).

models, lent themselves to a similar metamorphosis.

Les Parisiens à Cherbourg . . . (Fig. 51), drawn on a hot August day, spans the gap between realism and surrealism. Come summer, Parisians left for the country, and the well-to-do flocked to seaside resorts. In mid-century provincial inns offered the only shelter available to the vacationer. When the few rooms were filled, beds crowded the corridors, tents spotted the lawns. Indeed the local inhabitants, left throughout the winter to their own meager resources, felt no compunction whatever in making hay while the sun shone.

If we are to believe Daumier, even staircases were put to profitable use, each lodger being alloted an individual step. In *Les Parisiens à Cherbourg*, two men in night attire attempt sleep on such Spartan beds. Their clothes hang on pegs. For furnishings, a candle, a washbasin, a water jug. "Place for six roomers more," adds the caption. Thus the gist of the story-telling. Our specialized interest focuses here on the smoothness with which Daumier has transformed the tawdry staircase into a fabulous architecture. It spirals upward without visible support and without visible end, reminiscent of the ribbon of bronze reliefs that wraps itself diagonally around the Trajan Column, Daumier's classical favorite.

Art and folk-art sources of motion

Though the present study does not feature the usual art historical comparisons, mapping the climate that surrounded Daumier will help us place his work in perspective. His relationship to the Barbizon School, friendly if puzzled, has been touched upon, as well as his lyrical use of chiaroscuro for ends distinct from those of the realist school. As regards neoclassicism, what followers of Jacques-Louis David were still active had settled into routine teaching, striving to instill in schoolboys, plumbline in hand, the awe they felt at the sight of plaster Apollos, fig leaf and all (D. 1468). Though Daumier, in his cartoons, burlesques their cult of the antique, the thoughtful orderliness distilled out of his own compositions is proof enough that an unassuming classicism was indeed one of the ingredients of his complex style.

However, most "modern" art went another way. Following Delacroix, romantic rebels waved high their colorful banner. Had Daumier's oils been better publicized, he might have been counted one of them. Not that his graphics lean that way. When the vagaries of foreign politics brought Morocco into the headlines, Daumier sketched *mamamouchis* straight out of Molière, sucking on a narghile pipe and shaded by a dilapidated umbrella, indeed a far

Fig. 52. *Entrez donc, monsieur . . . ne vous gênez pas . . . c'est un tableau vivant! . . .* (Delteil 1538).

cry from Delacroix' Moresque magic (D. 1327). Nevertheless, unlike the balanced compositions we have studied, there are others, based on a willful disequilibrium, that show Daumier adapting to his own ends the dynamics that romantics favored. His preferred subjects, street scenes, artisans at their work, precluded the possibility of posed models. In his graphics he mocked colleagues who, with a system of cords and pulleys, froze the live model into postures meant to suggest motion (Fig. 52).

The flagstone pavement that David had set unyielding under the feet of the Horatii symbolized for neoclassical artists an immutable order. Newcomers, rating fluids over solids, chose to set their episodes on ever unstable waters. Literally so, be it the Styx on whose swift current Delacroix precariously launches Dante's skiff, or the high seas shredding to bits the raft of the Medusa and its load of derelicts. *Victor Hugo et Emile de Girardin cherchent à élever le Prince Louis* . . . (Fig. 53) mimics, not unkindly, Géricault's masterpiece. Wracked by political tempests, the future Napoleon III precariously attempts a sailor's stance on the tiniest of rafts.

Daumier's aversion to the picturesque limited the range of his dynamic ventures. His colleagues searched far and wide for heroic, tragic,

ACTUALITÉS.   Nº 171.

M.M. Victor Hugo et Emile Girardin cherchent à élever le prince Louis sur
un pavois, ça n'est pas très solide !

Fig. 53. *Victor Hugo et Emile de Girardin cherchent à
élever le Prince Louis . . .* (Delteil 1756).

or poetic subject matter. Daumier remained
content with the sights, noises, smells even, of
the Paris he loved. Tired of walking he would
climb on the omnibus, memorizing its motley
array of passengers and, more to our point, the
vagaries of its inner architecture. At stops, the
upright of the jambs, the row of rectangular
windows, the arched ceiling evoked stability.
On the go, thanks to rusty springs, reluctant
horses, and unpredictable street pavements,
coach and passengers alike suffered a metamorphosis, shaken up and down, thrown to the
right and to the left. *Intérieur d'un omnibus . . .*
Fig. 54) sets the plight of the damsel in such an
architecture in motion. Its verticals mimic diagonal postures, its horizontals shift like the
sea—until the next stop, when a more classical
order of things shall, for at least a moment, pre-
vail.

The hand puppets of the Champs-Elysées
had taught Daumier gestures more telling in
their staccato simplicity than those of live actors, a knowledge he memorized and used to
quicken the grasp of the readers of *Le Charivari*
on his graphic story-telling. Besides, tools in

Fig. 54. *Intérieur d'un omnibus. Entre un homme ivre et un charcutier* (Delteil 566).

daily use furnished him with patterns of mechanical motion. The grocer, the butcher weighed their goods on a pair of scales. At times the bourgeois, but more often his cook, basket in hand, watched closely the arm of this simple machine as it hovered hesitantly along diagonals, until both scales, their weight equalized, returned it to the horizontal. Daumier lifted this commercial tableau to a symbolic plane. One of the few lithographs that an ever-alert censor, smelling a shift in the political winds, rejected, it shows giant scales wherein the French Republic, a statuesque matron, outweighs a bunch of reactionary plotters (untitled, Deteil 2000, as *Suffrage universel*) (Fig. 55).

A nursery commonplace, the seesaw, motored by playful children into a sort of perpetual motion, inspired Daumier. *La Balançoire turco-russe* (Fig. 56) adapts it to headlines. Set on top of the pediment of this Temple of Mammon, La Bourse, a turbaned Turk and a Russian in furred hat keep the seesaw going to the dismay of puzzled investors.

Nouveau Joujou dédié par Ratapoil . . . (Fig. 57) taps an even humbler source. Since at least the eighteenth century, street peddlers hawked penny toys that today we would title "mobiles." Constructed of painted sticks moved by moppet power, two wrestlers wrestled, or two

Fig. 55. *Suffrage universel* (Delteil 2000).

Fig. 56. *La Balançoire turco-russe* (Delteil 2506).

Fig. 57. *Nouveau Joujou dédié par Ratapoil . . .* (Delteil 2158).

smiths, face to face, hammered at their forge. Here Ratapoil, his mustache bristling upright not unlike demon's horns, is the toy hawker. *En lieu* of smiths, evil politicians, each armed with Guignol's own bludgeon, administer to the French Republic an endless bastinado.

Dynamic composition

To illustrate Daumier's fluctuating understanding of motion as an aesthetic means, we may compare two lithographs identical as to subject matter, drawn twelve years apart. In 1833, Daumier was in his mid-twenties and already well known, partly for his metamorphosis of the features of King Louis-Philippe into a pear, a visual prank that eventually put him in jail. *Le Bois est cher et les arts ne vont pas* (Fig. 58) dates from that same year. It is winter. In their studio two artists perform a joyless dance as an alternative to freezing. The story-telling is childishly explicit. A musician holds tight to his violin, while behind his music sheets are displayed on a stand. The painter, as he dances, hugs his loaded palette, brushes, and mahlstick. An open paintbox, an unfinished canvas set on an easel leave us in no doubt as to his vocation! The studio itself is overstuffed with bric-a-brac. On the walls, plaster casts, prints,

Fig. 58. *Le Bois est cher et les arts ne vont pas* (Delteil 146).

Fig. 59. *Quant on a brûlé son dernier chevalet* (Delteil 1334).

pictures. On a shelf, a potiche and a bust. On the floor made of rotted planking stand a plaster torso, a cold food warmer, dirty dishes. In the time it takes us to make this inventory the legs and arms of the personages, though angled to imitate motion, become weighted into motionlessness by such a load of anecdotal story-telling.

Quant on a brûlé son dernier chevalet (Fig. 59) is a second version of the identical subject. Drawn twelve years later, with the added experience of twelve hundred lithographs between, it shows how Daumier's ideas have evolved. As stated in the caption, all wooden stuff—furniture, easel, violin even—has been fed to the cylindrical stove. Factually a logical step and as well a pictorial boon, for the studio is now free of bric-a-brac. A single unfinished painting, mural in scale, leans against the whitewashed wall. The cold stove angles its pipe toward the ceiling. The two artists, as before, dance to avoid freezing, but now have plenty of knee and elbow room to move in. This second version seems a shorthand rendering of the first, but it is more than that. Instead of a dynamic

Fig. 60. *Le Carcan* (Delteil 105).

Fig. 61. *Un Procédé pour qu'il marche sans avancer* (Delteil 3645).

subject matter stifled by a static composition, subject matter and composition are now equally dynamic. The large painting leaning against the wall could be understood as the rectangle of the image area tipped off balance. The stovepipe propped against the upper corner of the image opposes its obtuse angle to the right angle of the border as if the latter had been disarticulated and set loose. Chiaroscuro, in the first version realistically rounding each object, acquires now a life all its own, its strokes the trails of the motion of Daumier's hand at work. Not only the humans, but the objects, canvas, stove, areas of light and dark, the animate and the inanimate, all dance!

In the preceding examples motion has been, in varying degrees, a consequence of the subject matter. The pair of scales, the seesaw, the penny toy, though lifted to a symbolic plane, were borrowed straight out of daily realities. The second version of the pair of studio scenes activated abstract relationships of lines and angles as an accompaniment to the human pantomime. Though it would be pleasant, given the taste of our time, to map Daumier's progress from realism to abstraction on the strength of these two studio scenes, facts are otherwise. Our next example, dissociating still further composition from subject matter, dates in fact from his early days as a cartoonist.

Le Carcan (Fig. 60)—as does Daumier's better-known masterpiece *Le Ventre Législatif*—pictures a meeting of the Chamber of Peers. In both prints the hemicycle is spattered with seated politicians, some impassive, some dozing so deeply that, as far as human motion is concerned, the whole could pass for a waxwork display. Caught in frontal view, *Le Ventre Législatif* is eminently static. *Le Carcan*, focusing on the same scene from the side, features the hall itself, summing up the stepped-up rows of benches as concentric segments of circles with the speaker's podium as their common center. The strong set of perspective curves flows forward with such force that, leaping over the edges of the image, it spreads far and wide, suggesting a giant roulette wheel in motion. As drawn, the story is static, the composition dynamic.

Un Procédé pour qu'il marche sans avancer (Fig. 61), a late "Gillotage," includes a similarly circular motion as part of a clumsy piece of machinery, a stone mill. A blind Rosinante named Progress, harnessed to the handle of the grinding stone, plods dispiritedly along a circular track, her slow tempo contrasting with the swift flow conjured in *Le Carcan*. Though perpetual motion is the gist of the story, the composition remains static.

Fig. 62. *Les Trains de Plaisir. Quand après dix assauts infructueux . . .* (Delteil 3295).

Fig. 63. *Aspect que commencent déjà à avoir chaque soir les rues . . .* (Delteil 2931).

Toward infinity

Most of Daumier's compositions even, as we have just observed, when they involve circular motion, cover limited areas. Daumier's land-scapist friends had all freedom to put between them and the segment of nature they fancied such distance that even the hastiest of sketches encompassed vast vistas. Conscious of being one ant in the human ant hill, Daumier had nei-ther the ways nor the wish to insulate himself from his models in this fashion. Observation at close range spelled a close composition. In his scarce sorties out of these chosen limits he cau-tiously refuses to discard those familiar figures, the rectangle and the cube.

Les Trains de Plaisir . . . (Fig. 62) deals with city dwellers overcrowding so-called pleasure trains, the quicker to escape summer's stifling heat. The low line of sight makes the assaulted train loom formidable, yet, on analysis, what Daumier has drawn is little more than a reced-ing series of doors opening on the compart-ments, a set of parallel rectangles diminishing in scale, drawn a bold black in the foreground and modulated, according to the laws of aerial perspective, to delicate grays as they recede, or so it appears to us, into infinity.

Daumier's other standard unit, the cube, stands throughout his graphics as the basic summary for a Paris apartment. *Aspect que com-mencent déjà à avoir chaque soir les rues . . .* (Fig. 63) aligns side by side and piles on top of each other these symbols of the Parisians' tenuous privacy. For each unit dwellers rush simultane-ously to identical balconies, hoping for a first glimpse of the comet that is making headlines. The magic of aerial and linear perspective stretches this dismal sight even further than the length of a Paris street, ad infinitum.

In England, in the 1840s, J. W. Turner in *Rain, Steam and Speed* had portrayed the newly har-nessed steam power as an iron steed belching soot, a locomotive noisily straddling a peaceful Thames. Equally awed by this dubious inven-tion, Daumier hints more gently at its destruc-tive power. In *Oh! Le gueux . . .* (Fig. 64), as the iron monster surges over the horizon, a hunter watches impotently the imminent destruction of the hare he has just shot and who chose to die over the steel tracks. So unswerving are the bare perspective lines rushing straight at the viewer that one imperceptibly moves sideways to escape a similar fate.

Fig. 64. *Oh! Le gueux . . . il a été mourir là exprès . . .* (Delteil 2889).

Fig. 65. *Position réputée la plus commode pour avoir un joli portrait . . .* (Delteil 1525).

Fig. 66. *Souvenirs* (Delteil 579).

Fig. 67. *Comment se termine, après dîner, une conversation conjugale* (Delteil 1498).

Fig. 68. *Prison royale—Entrée—Sortie* (Delteil 209).

Varied approaches to time.

Even before the mid-century, Daumier, who could not even in a portrait detach form from motion or motion from time, felt uneasy at the potential of yet another invention, the daguerreotype. *Position réputée la plus commode pour avoir un joli portrait . . .* (Fig. 65) parallels his satirical sketch about painters who, with a system of ropes and pulleys, froze the nude model into a pose meant to depict action (Fig. 52). Here the racking with stems and screws that the sitter patiently endures to win pictorical immortality is funny, but unfunny is the goal of the wizard draping himself within the machine. As his chemical brews acquire potency, the photographer will reduce the time of pose to little or nothing, and thus snap totally unnatural images of man disconnected from time's flow, with all traces of motion eliminated.

The daguerreotype was part of a concerted assault on dynamic mysteries that would better have been left alone. Scientists disturbed time's

flow in yet another way, by clocking phases of motion so minutely that a past action could be artificially reanimated. From the 1830s on, primitive forms of cinematography were worked into toys, the phenakistoscope that revolved vertically, the zoetrope that revolved horizontally. His eye fixed to a minute lookout, the viewer watched birds in flight, balls bouncing, frogs jumping. Boys pedaled their velocipedes, girls skipped rope. Such a timing of motion by the clock clashed with Daumier's idea of a time that quickened or slowed down according to man's moods. The passionate oratory of a prosecutor, flailing space with as many arms as a Hindu god, hurried time. Evenings, time slowed to a stop when the bourgeois, dropping his newspaper to the carpet, dozed. In the lithographs, Time dons varied masks. A time clocked by the calendar, as the Old Year slinks away and the New Year 1842 is joyfully greeted (D. 976). It may be time remembered, as the aged roué lulls himself to sleep contemplating the portrait of his young mistress, young that is when rococo was in its prime (Fig. 66). Not even hinted at in the caption, time is wordlessly present as a well-fed couple in well-padded armchairs, resting their hands over their bellies, sit under portraits, his and hers, that resembled them twenty years ago (Fig. 67).

A drastic manipulation of time is featured in an early pen-and-ink lithograph, *Prison royale—Entrée—Sortie* (Fig. 68). Compositionally it remains unique in Daumier's work in that it presents the primary cube sideways, its corner jutting forward within the rectangle that frames the image. The jail building looms menacingly like the prow of a dreadnought of stone. On the left the prisoner enters. On the right he leaves, a corpse boxed in a pauper's coffin. What happened in between, boredom, starvation, sickness, despair, is left out. All intermediate episodes, in film parlance, have been strewn on the floor of the cutting room. Only these two moments, initial and terminal, are seen spliced together.

Jean Charlot (1898-1979) worked as a liturgical artist and writer in Paris before moving to Mexico in 1920. There he worked as a printmaker and painted the first monumental fresco in modern times, which became a technical, thematic, and stylistic influence on the Mexican mural renaissance. He also worked as an archaeologist and wrote extensively on all periods of Mexican art history including the first article on José Guadalupe Posada.

Moving to the United States in 1930, Charlot continued his work as artist and scholar, teaching at several universities. In 1949, he moved to Hawaii, where he produced murals and monumental sculpture in several media and wrote on various aspects of Hawaiian culture and history.

Honoré Daumier, photograph by Nadar, c. 1870. The International Museum of Photography at George Eastman House, Rochester, N.Y.

Donna Stein

Daumier: Photography and the Demand for Contemporaneity

hilosophically determined "to be of his own time,"[1] Honoré Daumier was one of the first artists to chronicle the new vogue for photography less than a year after Daguerre announced his process to the French Academy of Science on 19 August 1839. From 1840 to 1865, when government censorship forced Daumier to turn from political to social satire, he occasionally caricatured photographic subjects. He produced eleven lithographs and two wood engravings; two drawings are also attributed to his hand. These works represent, however, only a small sampling of his enormous graphic production and, in general, lack the passion and comedy that pervade so much of his other production.

Though Daumier was quick to respond to the new medium, he showed himself unconvinced of its validity and usefulness. Through the titles of his caricatures and his distinctive graphic humor, he sarcastically questioned whether photography was indeed an art or merely a mechanical procedure. According to Charles Blanc, founder of *Gazette des Beaux-Arts*, Daumier declared: "Photography imitates everything and expresses nothing—it is blind in the world of the spirit."[2] In his sketches, Daumier communicates his inherent distrust of the new invention and reveals his lack of foresight. He was untouched by the artistic potential of photography during this period and focused on the technical limitations of the medium, the professional pretense of the photographers, and the self-adulation of the well-to-do bourgeoisie.

In the early days of photography, lengthy sittings with exposure times from twenty seconds to twenty minutes were a serious restriction. *La patience est la vertu des ânes*, 1840 (Fig. 1), the third lithograph in the series *Proverbes et Maximes*, is a wry comment on the long exposure times required to produce a successful picture. For this first essay on photography, Daumier drew a sceptic leaning against the parapet of a quay observing the photographer, who, with watch in hand, patiently awaits the exact moment to snap the lens of his camera. Undoubtedly, the photographer represents Daguerre and, although the camera is pointed toward the opposite bank of the Seine, the other man is probably an impatient customer.[3]

One of the refinements fabricated to position, steady, and support the sitter was the headrest, which became standard equipment in a photographer's studio. The apparatus was attached to elaborate chairs on platforms with revolving seats for greater mobility and flexibility. Posing became an art in itself. Daumier's eye exposed the deceitful practices of photographers. In two lithographs, he ridicules these devices, which resembled medieval instruments of torture and often imparted an undesirable stiffness to the sitter: *Position réputée la plus commode . . .*, 1847 (see Charlot, Fig. 65), and *Photographie: Nouveau procédé. . .*, 1856 (Fig. 2). The earlier caricature, plate 49 from the series *Les Bons Bourgeois*, takes place on the terrace of a photography studio; a man, his head clamped into position, is uncomfortably seated in front of the camera waiting to be photographed. In the later lithograph, from the *Croquis Parisiens* series, the photographer motions to a seated couple, holding hands and posing with comic gravity, not to move. The motif of the headrest appears again

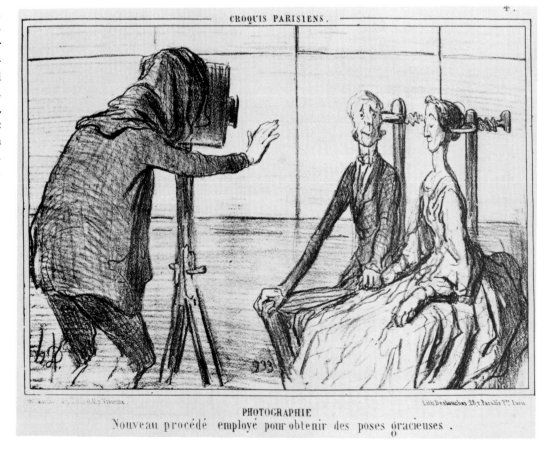

M. PRUDHOMME DEVANT L'OBJECTIF

Fig. 3. Honoré Daumier, *M. Prudhomme devant l'objectif* [M. Prudhomme in front of the camera], n.d., charcoal drawing. Formerly Collection Nadar. Present location unknown.

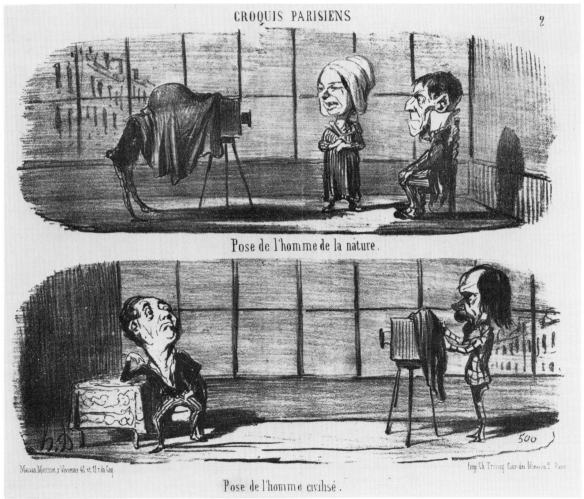

Fig. 4. Honoré Daumier, *Pose de l'homme de la nature. Pose de l'homme civilisé* [Pose of the country type. Pose of the civilized type], lithograph. *Le Charivari,* 31 March 1853 (H. D. 1474; D. 2445). The International Museum of Photography at George Eastman House, Rochester, N.Y.

Posant en membre du comice d'Agriculture de son département.

Fig. 5. Honoré Daumier, *Posant en membre du comice d'Agriculture de son département* [Posing as a member of the agricultural commission of his department], lithograph. *Le Charivari*, 30 January 1865 (H. D. 950; D. 3416). The Metropolitan Museum of Art, Rogers Fund, 1922.

in *M. Prudhomme devant l'objectif*, n.d. (Fig. 3), a drawing attributed to Daumier and formerly in the collection of Nadar.[4]

In two lithographs and two wood engravings, Daumier mocks human vanity in front of the camera. He unmasked both patrons and photographers. In a sheet with double-view scenes from *Croquis Parisiens*, Daumier contrasts two types of personality: *Pose de l'homme de la nature* and *Pose de l'homme civilisé*, 1853 (Fig. 4). The photographer's studio is the setting for both scenes. In the upper section, a farmer and his wife pose in front of the camera. The stern-looking man is rigidly seated with his hands on his knees, while his wife stands benignly, slightly in front of him, resting her crossed arms on her stomach. Below, a pompous-looking tailor, with his chest thrust forward, leans his elbow on a table covered with an oriental rug. This confrontation of opposites is a common device and appears frequently in the social satire of the period. Daumier's last lithograph on a photographic theme is *Posant en membre du comice d'Agriculture. . .* , 1865 (Fig. 5), from *Les Bons Bourgeois*. Here, the photographer aims the camera at a self-satisfied middle-class man, who is leaning against the wall of a garden terrace. He holds a shovel and stands next to a watering can, the attributes of his vocation. The sitter grimaces at the camera in *Beim Photographen*, 1842 (Fig. 6), one of the vignette wood engravings illustrating *Un Voyage d'Agréments à Paris*, published by the Musée Philipon in 1842. The same theme of vainglorious pride is seen again in *Photographes et Photographies*; the wood engraving by Charles Maurand (Fig. 7) was reproduced in *Le Monde Illustré* (29 March 1862). A lost drawing (Fig. 8) for this illustration attributed to Daumier has recently surfaced from a private collection in Paris.[5] At the time, these caricatures may have served as relevant lessons in humility and honesty.

Another pair of lithographs illustrates the ignorance and narrowmindedness of the bourgeoisie and shows how ill-informed it was about photography. In *Tiens, ma femme. . .* , 1846 (Fig. 9), plate 28 from *Les Bons Bourgeois*, an old man, just returned from a trip, stands in front of his opened suitcase and proudly exclaims to his wife, who stands at his side holding a portrait in her hands: "See, wife, here is my daguerreotype portrait that I've brought you from Paris. . . ." Naively, she complains: "Why didn't you have mine made at the same time . . . go on, you egoist." In another scene, *Papa contemplant l'image de son image*, 1847 (Fig. 10), plate 40 from *Les Bons Bourgeois*, Daumier portrays a proud father, seated in profile view, looking with satisfaction at a daguerreotype portrait of his baby son; a nursemaid with the child in her arms stands at his side.

388. Beim Photographen

Fig. 6. After Honoré Daumier, *Beim Photographen* [At the photograph], wood engraving. *Un Voyage d'Agrements à Paris,* 1842 (Fuchs 388).

Photographes et photographiés. (Dessin de M. Daumier.)

Fig. 7. Charles Maurand, after Honoré Daumier, *Photographes et Photographiés* [Photographer and photographed], wood engraving. *Le Monde Illustré,* 29 March 1862 (Fuchs 482). The International Museum of Photography at George Eastman House, Rochester, N.Y.

Fig. 8. Honoré Daumier, attributed to, untitled, n.d., charcoal and sepia wash drawing (7⅞ x 9⁹/₁₆ in.). Thackrey & Robertson, San Francisco, Calif.

Fig. 9. Honoré Daumier, *Tiens, ma femme, v'là mon portrait au Daguerréotype que je te rapporte de Paris. . . ./Pourquoi donc est-ce que tu n'as pas aussi fait faire le mien pendant que tu y étais? . . . égöiste va! . . .* , lithograph. *Le Charivari*, 7 December 1846 (H. D. 881; D. 1504). The Metropolitan Museum of Art, Gift in Honor of Kathleen W. Naef, 1978.

LES BONS BOURGEOIS.

N.º 40.

954

Papa contemplant l'image de son image.

Fig. 10. Honoré Daumier, *Papa contemplant l'image de son image* [Father contemplating the image of his image], lithograph. *Le Charivari*, 14 April 1847 (H. D. 893; D. 1516). The International Museum of Photography at George Eastman House, Rochester, N.Y.

Les Etrangers à Paris.

16.

643

Fig. 11. Honoré Daumier, *Le Portrait au Daguéréotype: Voila le produit du soleil. . . , comme c'est coloré, hein? . . . comme c'est chaud . . . et en trois secondes!/Eh!ben vrai. . . . on ne dirait pas en voyant ça que je ne suis resté que trois secondes au soleil. . . . on croirait plutôt que j'y ai demeuré trois ans, car j'ai l'air d'un véritable nègre . . . ça ne fat rien, c'est un joli portrait, et ma femme sera bien contente!*, lithograph. *Le Charivari*, 11 August 1844 (H. D. 1726; D. 1287). Prints Division, The New York Public Library, Astor, Lenox and Tilden Foundations.

Intérieur d'un magasin de St Petersbourg, pris au Daguerréotype en 1854.

Fig. 12. Honoré Daumier, *Intérieur d'un magasin de St Petersbourg, pris au Daguerréotype en 1854* [Interior of a store in St. Petersburg, daguerreotype prize in 1854], lithograph. *Le Charivari*, 23 December 1854 (H. D. 3052; D. 2538). The Metropolitan Museum of Art, Gift of Harry Friedman, 1954.

The commercial aspects of the new art commodities are examined in three lithographs. In *Le Charivari* of 11 August 1844, Daumier published *Le Portrait au Daguéréotype . . .* (Fig. 11), plate 16 from the series *Les Etrangers à Paris*. A man accompanied by his young son puts his hand in his pocket to pay for the daguerreotype portrait that the photographer holds before him with a triumphant air saying: "Here is the product of the sun . . . look at its tone . . . well done . . . and in three seconds." The man answers: "Well, it is the truth . . . one wouldn't say in seeing this that I only remained in the sun for three seconds . . . instead one would think that I had stayed there three years, because I look like a black man . . . that doesn't change anything, it is a pretty portrait and my wife will be delighted." Ten years later, for *Intérieur d'un magasin. . . ,* 1854 (Fig. 12), Daumier drew two dejected, melancholic men seated in a shop that sells novelties. Presumably, they didn't have any customers for their photographic services. For *En Amateur—Mais quel est donc ce tableau. . . ,* 1859 (Fig. 13), a caricature from *La Salle des Ventes*, Daumier reproduced a room in the Hôtel Druout in which absorbed-looking collectors and dealers, seated at a table, are carefully scrutinizing a framed picture held for them by the auctioneer. The collector says: "But is this a painting . . . I don't see anything except black?" The auctioneer replies: "It is a daguerreotype of the emperor Soulouque."

Nadar élevant la Photographie. . . , 1862 (Fig. 14), surpasses all of Daumier's other compositions with photographic themes in the sophistication and complexity of its visual information and in the broad ramifications of its intellectual content.[6] It was published in *Le Boulevard*, a weekly magazine founded by Etienne Carjat, writer, caricaturist, photographer, and friend of the artist.

Daumier portrays the flamboyant Nadar (Gaspard-Felix Tournachon) rising above the city of Paris in his balloon, the "Giant." For comic effect the artist accentuated expressive gestures and dispensed with accurate detail. We no longer see the enclosed nacelle of the original craft. By placing the photographer in a basketlike contraption, he was able to show Nadar with his Dallmeyer camera attached to a tripod and focused on the city below. In point of fact, Nadar never used a tripod for aerial photography; he either attached the camera to the side of the basket or put the lens through the bottom.[7] In the foreground plane, all the buildings have "photography" lettered across them. The repeated use of the word implies that each house in Paris also accommodated a photographic trade and profession.

Here, for the first time, Daumier identifies an actual personality among the early French

Fig. 13. Honoré Daumier, *En Amateur—Mais quel est donc ce tableau . . . on n'y voit rien que du noir? . . ./Le Crieur—C'est l'empereur Soulouque tiré au daguerréotype,* lithograph. *Le Charivari,* 16 March 1859 (H. D. 2513; D. 3129).

photographers and pays double homage to his friend, the celebrated photographer and daredevil astronaut. Yet he also mocks Nadar's insistent showmanship and, in the title for the caricature, subtly puns his self-advertisement as a "photographer of art." This broadside appeared shortly after the publicity of the famous Mayer and Pierson court case of 1861-62, which resolved the status of photography as an independent art in the affirmative. Nonetheless, Daumier was the first artist among his contemporaries to acknowledge Nadar's extraordinary feat in the autumn of 1858, when, after four previous failures, and using the cumbersome wet-plate process, he successfully made a clear photograph from the cabin of his balloon showing the French countryside outside Paris. Daumier also comments on the dramatic vista of the city seen from above, a point of view that aerial photography and the concurrent vogue for Japanese art naturally advanced, and one

that decisively influenced the impressionists' new and unusual bird's-eye view of a metropolis.

Daumier, twelve years Nadar's senior, was something of a father figure for the younger artist. Their lives show a certain parallelism of thought and action: Daumier, born in Marseille, left for Paris in his youth; Nadar, Parisian-born, spent his old age in Marseille. As ardent republicans, they were politically congenial and probably met when they were both working as caricaturists for *Le Charivari.* Both recorded Parisian life with a similar comprehensive approach; Nadar's photographs and Daumier's paintings and lithographs reflect their mutual research and experimentation into unusual tonal effects produced by artificial lighting. Nadar was a member of a committee, headed by Victor Hugo, of thirty distinguished people in the world of arts and letters. In October 1877, this group arranged the first retro-

Fig. 14. Honoré Daumier, *Nadar élevant la Photographie à la hauteur de l'Art* [Nadar elevating photography to artistic heights]. *Le Boulevard,* 25 May 1862 (H. D. 243; D. 3248). The Metropolitan Museum of Art, Harris Brisbane Dick Fund, 1926.

spective of Daumier's art in Paris from April to June 1878 at the prestigious Galeries Durand-Ruel.

More than seventy portraits in every media exist of Daumier by his friends, including Corot, Daubigny, Pascal, Henri Monnier, Feuchère, Bernais, and Hadol. Nadar first recorded his friend in two drawings of about 1850 and 1852. He also copied one of Daumier's "Ratapoil" compositions.[8] In 1855, just two years after Nadar began to photograph seriously, he shot at least four three-quarter portraits of Daumier, his hair and beard beginning to gray, wearing an undistinguished topcoat. The pictures were probably commissioned by Daumier because of his participation that year in the first Parisian Universal Exposition. Evidently, in appreciation and exchange for his services, Nadar became the first owner of a *Don Quixote* grisaille painting. Shortly before Daumier died, Nadar photographed him again, in about 1877; the portrait was printed as a woodburytype reproduction in the *Galerie Contemporaine*. By then, Daumier was old, poor, and blind, but he appears more prosperous than in the earlier portraits and is dressed in a fashionable suit. He was also photographed by Pierre Petit and Etienne Carjat.

Daumier, who had an uncanny ability to remember, stylize, and interpret essential form, never painted or drew from life. Thus, unlike many of his contemporaries, he had no direct personal use for photography. Furthermore, the publications for which he worked did not employ photographic reproductions on a regular basis until after his death in 1879. Like so many of his contemporaries, Daumier feared that photography would supplant the other arts in effectiveness and popularity.

Working as he did in black and white, Daumier limits detail and symbolically and tonally juxtaposes form to clearly project content. The simple, economical construction of his compositions suggests the "decisive moment," when all elements are in balance. His odd angles, unusual points of view, and selective framing are dependent on the unique qualities of camera vision. No artist, including Daumier, could remain impervious to the ways photography has penetrated and influenced our minds and our vision.

Notes

1 "Il faut être de sons temps" is one of the few authenticated statements of the artist and the slogan of the Romantic philosophers, the radical realist artists led by Courbet, and the impressionists who came after Manet.

2 Heinrich Schwarz, "Daumier, Gill and Nadar," *Gazette des Beaux-Arts*, 49, February 1957, p. 99.

3 Ibid.

4 Emile Dacier, "La Photographie à travers l'image," *Annuaire Général et International de la Photographie*, 14, 1905, p. 16.

5 My sincere thanks to Charles Moffett, associate curator, Department of European Paintings, The Metropolitan Museum of Art, New York, who brought the drawing to my attention.

6 The second state of this lithograph was included in the journal *Souvenirs d'Artistes*.

7 Peter Pollack, *The Picture History of Photography from the Earliest Beginnings to the Present Day*, New York, 1977, p. 47.

8 Jean Cherpin, "'L'Homme Daumier': Un Visage qui sort de l'ombre," *Arts et Livres de Provence*, 87, 1973, p. 152.

Donna Stein, an independent critic and curator, is a Ph.D. candidate at the Institute of Fine Arts, New York University.

Fig. 1. Honoré Daumier, *Henri de Larochejacquelein,* lithograph. *Le Charivari,* 2–3 January 1849 (D.1808).

Fig. 2. Thomas Nast, *Bluebeard of New Orleans,* 1863, wash drawing made into carte-de-visite. The New-York Historical Society, New York.

Francine Tyler

The Impact of Daumier's Graphics
on American Artists: c.1863–c.1923

Both American political cartoonists and realist artists came under the influence of Daumier's art, which could turn from passionate political engagement to a compelling, witty, and clearsighted look at the social scene. To understand the full measure of Daumier's impact, however, it is necessary to remember that his milieu was not so different from that of the Americans he has inspired over the years. Even today, in economics, politics, social customs, and human behavior, there are parallels with his period: wives and husbands still misunderstand each other, tenants and landlords still battle, city blight still pushes into the country, swindlers still prey on the guilible, men and women still go to prison or die behind barbed wire or in battle, and military budgets mount ever higher; the Bar, the Stock Exchange, the medical profession, the stage, the fashion industry—all still deserve the watchful eye of the critic or commentator.[1]

Daumier's career owes everything to the amalgamation of caricature and journalism that was first begun in 1830 by Charles Philipon in Paris (*La Caricature* [1830–1835] and *Le Charivari* [1832–1913]) for the purpose of interpreting and criticizing government and society in pictures as well as in words. Through his newspapers, which can be called the parents of all future satiric journals, Philipon initiated Daumier's lifework and nurtured its development. Henry James wrote that journalism was felt to be the greatest invention of the age: "[It was] criticism of the moment *at* the moment and caricature is that criticism at once simplified and intensified by a plastic form,"[2] so that journalists and caricaturists assumed importance as the historians of their epoch. But the American journalists, James pointed out,

had not yet developed this critical insight. Their country was so raw and new, without a tradition to draw upon, that they could only propagate the news.[3] If they wished to probe deeper, they had to turn to Europe for advice.

A persuasive influence from across the Atlantic was Daumier, whose lithographs and wood engravings were published in various journals on an average of twice a week for forty years. With this kind of dissemination, he could not help but influence the French and foreign artists who encountered his drawings in the daily and weekly press. His presence lingered: long after his death his work in *Charivari* could be bought for three cents a page in the old print shops in Paris.[4]

"Delacroix copied Goya and Daumier, Manet did the same thing, and Degas knew his Daumier by heart," said William Ivins.[5] Other artists who came under Daumier's sway were recalled by Mahonri Young: "As an influence Daumier is to be seen in many men. Over certain black and white artists his spirit glows with a beneficent effulgence. We need only mention Forain, Steinlen and Boardman Robinson."[6] Artists and critics discerned the significance of Daumier and his fellow caricaturists who, in truly depicting their own time, broke through romantic and personal barriers of artistic isolation; what they achieved is best described by Richard Muther:

Whilst the world was laughing and crying, the painter, with the colossal power of doing everything, amused himself by trying not to appear the child of this time. No one perceived the refinement and grace, the corruption and wantonness, of modern life as it is in great cities. No one laid hold on the mighty social problems which the growing century threw out with a seething creative force. Whoever wishes to

Fig. 3. Honoré Daumier, *C. H. Odilon Barrot*, lithograph. *Le Charivari*, 17 January 1849 (D. 1813).

know how the men of the time lived and moved, what hopes and sorrows they bore in their breasts, whoever seeks for works in which the heart-beat of the century is alive and throbbing, must have his attention directed to the works of the draughtsmen, to the illustrations of certain periodicals.[7]

As an editorial cartoonist, Daumier sharpened the public's views on issues that were important to it. He had to think up a grand visual idea to turn double-dealing, stupidity, or corruption in government into a single, strong picture. His witty notions were often the suggestions of his editor, Philipon, his colleagues, or taken from the actions of characters in literature or the theater.

Thomas Nast (1840–1902), the father of American caricature, was as serious as Daumier about social and political causes and also adapted various sources, including, I believe, some of Daumier's caricatures, to achieve his inventive cartoons. Nast's career as an artist-journalist began with the establishment of *Frank Leslie's Illustrated Weekly Newspaper* (founded in 1855), for which he drew the news of the day—fires, prize fights, ships' dockings, and the like. *Harper's Weekly* (founded in 1857) hired him in 1862, during the American Civil War, and gave him the opportunity to be a commentator rather than an illustrator; he expressed his support of the Union cause in large, patriotic drawings suffused with homely pathos. In the era of Reconstruction that followed, a new kind of pictorial journalism was needed to expose those whose reactionary policies went against his radical republican principles. Nast abandoned his sentimental style and developed into a merciless editorial cartoonist, using the evaluative skills he had developed, the pen-and-ink linear style of the English illustrators, and the sharp, satiric exposure tactics of the French cartoonists, notably Daumier. Like them, Nast ridiculed his targets, placing them in fanciful attitudes, circumstances, and disguises.

No written statement is known that tells us that Nast, in his early career, was aware of Daumier's work, but there is some visual evidence and some circumstantial evidence to show that he did. The model for an early caricature by Nast, the pro-General Butler takeoff, must have been Daumier's *Henri de Larochejacquelein*, 1849 (Fig. 1). Butler, with flowing hair and in a similar pose and oriental costume, is depicted as the *Bluebeard of New Orleans*, 1863 (Fig. 2)—a satiric response to the British outcry against the general's order to form regiments of emancipated slaves to fight against the Confederacy and other orders when he was the commander of the victorious Union forces over New Orleans. Nast's drawing was photographed and mounted on heavy paper stock in calling-card format.[8] These cartes-de-visite portraits were very popular and avidly collected.[9]

Henri de Larochejacquelein is one in a series of Daumier caricatures of the parliamentarians of the Second Republic called *Les Représentans Représentés* which appeared in *Le Charivari* from November 1848 through August 1850. The artist used the antique device of big head on little body to convey, through subtle facial characterization, pose, gesture, and clothing, his approval or disapproval of his subject in a perceptive but comparatively understated way. The facial caricature is highly individualized and Nast adopted this kind of portrait caricature, in a milder manner, for his subsequent cartoons. It seems likely that Nast knew of or saw this series, because the political editor of *Harper's Weekly*, George William Curtis, lived in Paris in the winter of 1848–1849 when these pictures were appearing. *Henri de Larochejacquelein* was issued on January 3, 1849. Surely Curtis would have alerted Nast to the work of that successful and remarkable French caricaturist.

To see how clever Daumier's portrait caricatures are, compare two other lampoons in the series: *C. H. Odilon Barrot*, 1849 (Fig. 3), who became chief minister under Louis-Napoleon, is presented on a pedestal, hand in coat like a little dictator, a disapproving, fanatic look on his face; the suavely elegant banker *Léon Faucher*, 1849 (Fig. 4), exudes hypocrisy, duplicity, and disdain.

Andrew Johnson was Nast's first target. A "loyal War Democrat" as vice president under Lincoln, Johnson became an advocate of states' rights and white supremacy when elected to the presidency. In the same manner as Daumier, Nast caricatures Johnson, 1866 (Fig. 5), as a mean, unthinking pygmy, vehemently kicking out a bureau containing the freedmen, which, in fact, he did by his veto of 1866. The Bureau of Refugees, Freedmen, and Abandoned Lands, set up to consolidate the various Civil War departments specializing in Negro affairs, was praised by historian W. E. B. DuBois as "A government guardianship for the relief and guidance of white and black labor from a feudal agrarianship to modern farming and industry."[10] Nast copied photographs or drew from life for the likenesses of the people he caricatured, never exaggerating the truth too much so they would be instantly recognizable to the public.

For his most brilliant cartoons, Nast took on big city graft and the boss system in the person of William Marcy Tweed. The *"Brains,"* 1871 (Fig. 6), is captioned: "That Achieved the Tammany Victory at the Rochester Democratic Convention." Nast has changed Boss Tweed's head into a moneybag, marked with a dollar symbol, just as Philipon and Daumier had changed the head of Louis-Philippe into a pear (*poire* also meant fool). The "poire" libel by

Fig. 4. Honoré Daumier, *Léon Faucher*, lithograph. *Le Charivari*, 5 May 1849 (D. 1843).

Fig. 5. Thomas Nast, *The Veto*, wood engraving. *Harper's Weekly*, 14 April 1866.

THE "BRAINS"

THAT ACHIEVED THE TAMMANY VICTORY AT THE ROCHESTER DEMOCRATIC CONVENTION.

Daumier and Philipon was famous or infamous: William Makepeace Thackeray, Nast's favorite author, had published the episode in 1840 in his article, "Caricatures and Lithography in Paris," which appeared in his book *The Paris Sketch Book of Mr. M. A. Titmarsh*. Also, Thackeray was popular in the United States; he had lectured here in 1853 and 1855 and became a good friend of George William Curtis. Nast had to have known about the pear. In both cartoons, the visual joke removes the screen of facial features and devastatingly turns the men into what or who they essentially represent. Nast's drawing symbolizes the power of big business to buy and to corrupt after the Civil War. Writing about this phenomenon, James Parton the famous biographer, Nast's cousin-in-law, close friend, and fellow republican, noted that "The press caught them at the full tide of their success, when the Tammany Ring, in fell alliance with a railroad ring, was confident of placing a puppet of its own in the Presidential chair."[11]

In 1868, the New York State Legislature passed a law making public funds available to private—mainly Catholic—schools and charitable institutions. Nast objected to the legislation as interference with the separation of church and state and as a future drain on the public school system. Nast's *Tilden's "Wolf at the Door, Gaunt and Hungry"* . . . , 1876 (Fig. 7), bears a striking similarity to Daumier's composition *La Réforme Electorale en Angleterre* . . . , 1866 (Fig. 8), in which a strong, eager, and brutish John Bull tries to force his way into a meeting of the British cabinet (the British public's demand to be allowed to vote). In Nast's print, the ugly, howling wolf (the bill) juts his head in the door as the children push against him with all their might. In the background, Uncle Sam reaches for his gun. (Nast's drawing is reversed in the wood engraving.) Daumier must have been sympathetic to the Englishman's aspiration for the vote, yet his John Bull is chauvinistically stupid-looking. Here, perhaps mistaking the real meaning of Daumier's cartoon, Nast brings into play only the effective composition; his door-pusher, unlike Daumier's, is the enemy.

The French caricaturists' works were becoming well known because of the many Americans who traveled back and forth from Paris after the Civil War. Some Americans collected their works, which could be bought in albums: James Parton knew a New Yorker who owned a collection of 1,000 satirical pictures published in Paris from the time of the Franco-Prus-

Fig. 6. Thomas Nast, *The "Brains." That Achieved the Tammany Victory at the Rochester Democratic Convention*, wood engraving. *Harper's Weekly*, 21 October 1871.

Fig. 7. Thomas Nast, *Tilden's "Wolf at the Door, Gaunt and Hungry."—Don't Let Him In,* wood engraving. *Harper's Weekly,* 16 September 1876.

sian War to the rise of the Paris Commune. All readers of *Harper's Monthly Magazine* in 1875 knew about Daumier because the periodical published a series of articles by James Parton called "Caricature and Other Comic Art in All Times and Many Lands," which devoted considerable space to French caricaturists, mainly Daumier. The series appeared in book form in 1877. Parton, who must have discussed this project with Nast, quotes from Thackeray's 1840 article and also describes many cartoons he had seen.

The career of Joseph Keppler (1838–1894), who also developed his ideas from many sources, including Daumier, differed from that of Nast, for Keppler was both a publisher of illustrated newspapers and a caricaturist for them. After publishing the short-lived *Die Vehme* in St. Louis in 1868, he came to New York in 1872 to work on *Frank Leslie's Illustrated Weekly Newspaper,* and went on, in 1876, to publish the German-language *Puck,* making it an English-language paper the following year.

Fig. 8. Honoré Daumier, *La Réforme Electorale en Angleterre. . . ,* lithograph. *Le Charivari,* 26 February 1866 (D. 3487). The Metropolitan Museum of Art, Gift of Harry G. Friedman, 1960.

Fig. 9. Joseph Keppler, *Ein moderner Sisyphus*, lithograph. *Puck*, April 1877. *Scrapbooks of Puck*. Prints Division, The New York Public Library, Astor, Lenox and Tilden Foundations.

At first, Keppler drew three full- or double-page cartoons for each issue, innovatively employing lithography instead of the ubiquitous wood engraving; he later changed from black-and-white to full-color lithography. Soon he was able to hire other artists, who met weekly to discuss ideas for picture editorials before any drawings were made. Early in his career, Keppler had started a library of pictorial clippings, and this practice was continued at *Puck*. Two copies of all illustrated papers were received each week, and pictures from one of them, to be used as sources for motifs, were cut out and catalogued for the *Puck* library.[12] The *Puck* artists were also inspired by paintings of the old masters: subjects such as "St. George and the Dragon" and "The Judgment of Paris" after Rubens can be identified as the derivation of some of their cartoons. Daumier must have been in the picture file; for example, Ralph Shikes noted that Keppler's *The Bosses of the Senate*, 1889, is a twist on Daumier's *Le Ventre Législatif*, 1834.[13] Another probable borrowing from Daumier is based on the Greek conception of futility—the myth of Sisyphus, the Corinthian king who was sentenced in Hades to roll eternally up a mountain a huge stone that will only roll back down again. Keppler's cartoon refers to the efforts of a recognizable Carl Schurz, who, as *Ein moderner Sisyphus*, 1877 (Fig. 9), had been trying for years to pass a Civil Service Reform Bill that would insure the appointment of qualified people to civil service jobs. The work appears to be based on *Comme Sisyphe*, 1869 (Fig. 10), Daumier's wry comment in 1869 on the state of the French budget. Keppler's *The Bosses of the Senate* is crowded with people and details after Daumier's early style of work; *Ein moderner Sisyphus* is based on Daumier's later style, in which a monumental, symbolic figure acts in the drama of life on a stark, bare stage.

Daumier's influence continued in the work of Art Young (1866–1943), whose *Early Art-School Drawing*, c. 1872(?) (Fig. 11), demonstrates Young's rebellion against the lifeless academic art training of the time. He shared this preference for observing real life with Daumier, who had ridiculed contemporary pseudoclassicism by depicting in 1842 a scrawny Pygmalion's delight when his lumpy statue Galatea comes to life before his eyes (Fig. 12). Young later wrote, "Without a keen curiosity no one can be an artist. And seeing what is unposed and unconscious in the actions of individuals or groups affords more inspiration than any formal posing or conscious parade."[14]

Young became aware of the work of the European caricaturists and sensed their importance to him when he went to study in Paris, about which he said, with reverence, "Here Doré, Daumier, Steinlen and Millet had worked. . . ."[15] Bouguereau, Young's teacher at

Fig. 10. Honoré Daumier, *Comme Sisyphe*, lithograph. *Le Charivari*, 25 February 1869 (D. 3694).

the Académie Julian, remarked that a drawing Young had made was too brutal. Young, who thought the criticism unjustified, later wrote, "I knew that Hogarth, Daumier, and Doré also had been brutal in portraying brutality and that caricature meant the ability to exaggerate."[16]

Young bought a small collection of Daumier lithographs while in Paris, and when he returned to New York, Joseph Keppler's son gave him Keppler's collection of prints and European magazines.[17] Young provided little information about this gift, but it is likely that some Daumiers were included. To give him the self-confidence and knowledge with which to defend his point of view in his cartoons, Young attended free night classes at Cooper Union in parliamentary law, oratory, and debate. The students discussed tariffs, immigration, women's suffrage, the public ownership of utilities, taxation, states' rights, and so on.[18] At the time, there was intense public interest in social questions and reform. Periodicals such as *Life*, *Puck*, *Judge*, and *McClures's Magazine* published articles and cartoons denouncing firetrap tenements, child labor, graft by public officials, sweatshops, exploitation of the poor, and conditions that bred tuberculosis. The suffering of the immigrants pouring into the city shocked Young into an awareness of the "realities of the human struggle."[19] He sided with the "have-nots," as did a number of cartoonists and urban realist painters. To criticize these conditions and to expose their causes, he helped to found the *Masses*, a radical, iconoclastic journal based on contemporary European models like *Simplicissimus*, *Jugend*, *Gil Blas*, and *Assiette du Beurre*.

Taking his cue from Daumier's *Gargantua*, 1831 (D. 34; see Morse, p. 35), Young depicts in *Eleven Hours a Day*, c. 1911(?) (Fig. 13), an obscenely fat factory owner being stuffed with profits earned by children working long hours in his factory. Unlike Daumier's Louis-Philippe, who expelled his loot in the form of bribes, this exploiter keeps on expanding.

Boardman Robinson (1876–1952) bought Daumier lithographs when he was in Paris in the 1890s. Later, he paid high tribute to Daumier, saying: "There was a man! He went right at form, working as one does in modeling. His drawing came, daily, directly and hot off

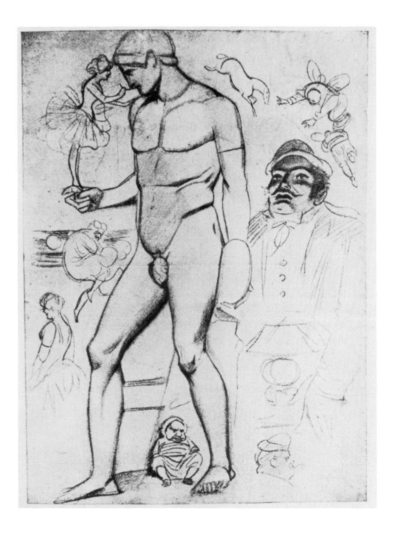

Fig. 11. Art Young, *Early Art-School Drawing*, c. 1872(?), charcoal drawing.

Fig. 12. Honoré Daumier, *Pygmalion* (from the series *Histoire Ancienne*), lithograph. *Le Charivari*, 28 December 1842 (D. 971). National Gallery of Art, Washington, D.C., Rosenwald Collection.

his mind. Here is another example where one cannot separate the man from the craft; Daumier was a great man."[20] About Robinson's achievement, a critic wrote in 1915 in *Vanity Fair:*

He killed the old, badly drawn cross-hatched line cartoon and developed a cartoon which was also a work of art. His big ideas and his big drawings have been reproduced more frequently in European papers than those of any other American artist. In method and grasp he belongs to the bold and simple school of Daumier. A few of his swift lines and a little of his grim sardonic humor are more deadly than columns of editorials.[21]

One of Robinson's most compelling works is *Europe—Mars and his constant companion survey the fertile field,* 1912 (Fig. 14), a sobering comment on the news that Turkey had declared war on Serbia and Bulgaria. Robinson was surely familiar with Daumier's last series of lithographs of the Franco-Prussian war, in which the helmeted figure of War and the skeleton of Death appear regularly. In Daumier's *Un Cauchemar de M. Bismark. . . ,* 1870 (Fig. 15), Death, unrobed and pointing his sharpened scythe at the battlefield of the slain, grins a hideous gratitude to the dreaming Bismarck, whose country was at war with France and exacting heavy losses.

To achieve Daumier's effect of a drawing done on stone, Robinson drew with crayon on a textured paper; the works were then photographically reproduced for the newspaper. He drew for the *New York Tribune* for many years, often commenting on the current social scene in his *New York Nuisances* series, for example, and in his drawings of American women enjoying the freedom of their new, loose clothing. The modern woman's fight for equal rights was usually ridiculed in cartoons, an attitude that perpetuated a lack of understanding of the contemporary woman and of her aims. Militant women especially were depicted as being indecorous, unfeminine, and inefficient. These characteristics are expressed in Robinson's *The Lady Hoodlums: English Suffragette. . . ,* 1911 (Fig. 16). The artist was unsympathetic to the English suffragettes who, imitating the historical methods of men, used civil disobedience and confrontation to help achieve the legislation they wanted. In *Ooray, Lizzie: Suffrage is defeated again!,* 1913 (*New York Tribune,* 8 May), Robinson tried to prove that those suffragettes who used violent methods were pleased when suffrage was defeated so they could continue making bombs and placing them in public buildings. Robinson's sketchy unkempt lines echo Daumier's late, loose drawing style, but his works have neither Daumier's control nor his insight into human behavior. After 1910, however, when the suffrage movement gained strength in the United States, Robinson por-

Fig. 13. Art Young, *Eleven Hours a Day*, c. 1911(?), pen and ink drawing.

Fig. 14. Boardman Robinson, *Europe–Mars and his constant companion survey the fertile field,* crayon drawing. *New York Tribune,* 18 October 1912.

Fig. 15. Honoré Daumier, *Un Cauchemar de M. Bismark.—Merci! . . . ,* lithograph. *Le Charivari,* 22 August 1870 (D. 3802).

Fig. 16. Boardman Robinson, *The Lady Hoodlums: English Suffragette*—"*Yes, mother, we have made a strong impression. They are beginning to realize the dignity of our movement,*" drawing. *New York Tribune*, 23 November 1911.

trayed American activists as polite ladies, always well dressed and smiling among male legislators. In these cartoons, he seems to be trying to persuade suffragettes to follow a certain mode of conduct.

Daumier, in approximately sixty plates on such topics as "Blue Stockings," "Divorcing Women," and "Female Socialists," had mocked French feminist behavior, thereby obscuring their deep commitment to their cause. Oliver Larkin feels, however, that Daumier was not against their ideas, but simply disliked some of the pretentious leaders of the movement.[22] In *Les Divorceuses. Toast porté à l'èmancipation des femmes. . .* , 1848 (Fig. 17), Daumier's women become manfully boisterous and disheveled as they toast their hoped-for emancipation. Frank Weitenkampf has shown that as soon as women in the United States began to strive for political and social rights they became targets of caricature by men who depicted them as mannish, loose, and inclined to drink.[23]

Another American admirer of Daumier was Robert Minor (1844–1952), who kept on his wall *Moderne Galilée*, 1834 (Fig. 18), one of Daumier's most moving works. It was drawn in 1834, when the pay rates of the Lyons silk workers were cut by the silk merchants; a sympathy strike in Paris was brutally suppressed by the government. This conflict, in which innocent people were jailed or murdered by government troops, led Daumier to create one of his greatest lithographs, *Rue Transnonain, Le 15 Avril 1834*, for *L'Association Mensuelle Lithographique*.

Moderne Galilée shows a prisoner in shirt sleeves sitting on a mat, his arms chained behind his back. The man is powerfully drawn and, as if a symbol of the one hundred men who were jailed during the strife, seems to be larger than life. Directly opposite stands Persil, the chief prosecutor, in his judicial robes. The cell is dark except for a blaze of light thrown on the wall by Liberty's torch, which reveals the years of struggle against an indifferent and unbearable regime—past, present, and future. Unlike the famous Italian astronomer, this Galileo refuses to recant. Minor produced a print in a

Fig. 17. Honoré Daumier, *Les Divorceuses. Toast porté à l'èmancipation des femmes. . .* , lithograph. *Le Charivari*, 12 October 1848 (D. 1773). Prints Division, The New York Public Library, Astor, Lenox and Tilden Foundations.

Fig. 18. Honoré Daumier, *Moderne Galilée*, lithograph. *La Caricature*, 6 November 1834 (D. 93). The
Metropolitan Museum of Art, Rogers Fund, 1918.

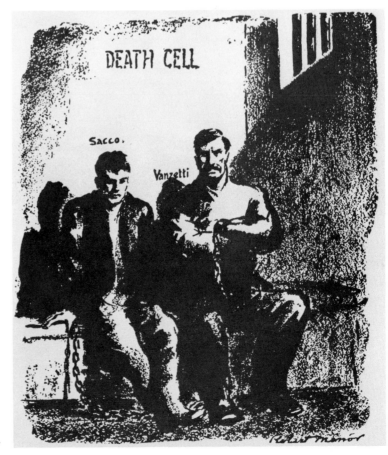

Fig. 19. Robert Minor, *Death Cell: Sacco and Vanzetti*,
c. 1923, drawing. International Publishers, New York.

similar vein to express his feelings about the
plight of Nicola Sacco and Bartolomeo Vanzetti
(who were in prison and later executed, ostensibly for a payroll robbery, but in Minor's view
and that of many others, for their radical be-
liefs). His print, c. 1923, less affecting than
Daumier's, depicts two chained men seated on
a bench in a death cell (Fig. 19). The prisoner on
the right resembles Daumier's jailed man. Light
streaming through the window across the wall
illuminates the faces of the prisoners and their
names and the words "death cell."

In the 1890s, the realist artists (who were
eventually labeled the "ashcan school") started
as artist-journalists for the illustrated
newspapers—a training ground in which they
discovered the vital poetry in ordinary life. The
realist artist was aptly defined by Frank Jewett

Fig. 20. Honoré Daumier, *Les Champs Elysées. Le Jeu de boules*, 1844, wood engraving. (Eugène Bouvy, *Daumier: L'Oeuvre Gravé du Maître*, Paris, 1933, I. no. 677). Prints Division, The New York Public Library, Astor, Lenox and Tilden Foundations.

Fig. 21. Honoré Daumier, *Révolution causée par une pluie d'orage, qui fond tout a coup sur les promeneurs. . .*, 1844, wood engraving (Eugène Bouvy, *Daumier: L'Oeuvre Gravé du Maître*, Paris, 1933, I. no. 686). Prints Division, The New York Public Library, Astor, Lenox and Tilden Foundations.

Mather, as one "who prefers discovering his beauty ready made in the world, and when he has ambushed it, lets it alone."[24] Unlike the academic artists of their day, the realists did not turn people into gods or goddesses or make their subjects vehicles for high moral statements or mythology. The best-known realist artists were Robert Henri, John Sloan, William Glackens, Everett Shinn, Jerome Myers, George Luks, Guy Pène du Bois, Eugene Higgins, George Bellows, and Glenn O. Coleman, all of whom owed a debt in some way to the precedent set by Daumier's relish for the character and life of Paris. At the time of the Armory Show in 1913, Glackens wrote: "Everything worthwhile in our art is due to the influence of French art. Our own art is arid and bloodless. It is nothing so much as dry bones. It shows that we are afraid to be impulsive, afraid to forget restraint, afraid above everything else to appear ridiculous."[25] In the emulation of the work of the French realists, Glackens saw the promise of a renaissance for American art.

As a friend or as an inspiring teacher, Robert Henri (1865–1929) introduced many Americans to Daumier. From Paris, in 1899, he sent Sloan some Daumier lithographs accompanied by a letter in which he wrote:

Are you interested in the work of Daumier—I am sending you . . . a few drawings (lithographs) by him—They came out in the "Charivari". I think about 25 years ago— . . . Daumier was a great painter as well as a draughtsman—there was one of his pictures "En Troisieme Class" view of a third class french RR carriage with wonderfully drawn or interpreted characters—most masterfully painted (none of the modern so highly esteemed clever smartness—but great solid simple painting). It is a picture that ranks at least with the best of Millets—and if they were side by side I might say more.[26]

Daumier's work expressed what Henri thought art should be: ". . . art must always deal with *life*, and it becomes significant as the ideas of the artist are significant. Art to every man must be his personal confession of life as he feels and knows it."[27] His students were advised to look at the prints of Daumier and those of the Japanese so they would notice the "mysteriously wonderful" qualities of life from which they could then choose aspects that quickened their own interest: "I have just noticed the backs of two little girls walking away. But there are so many I might notice. A woman in red with another at her side. Little children walking in parade. . . . Fat party in cab. . . . Sweepers. . . . People drooping in the rain. . . . And so forth, and so forth. All interesting matters of wit."[28] Henri spent many evenings at Sloan's house doodling little caricatures of people in Daumier's style.[29]

Henri was called "my father in art"[30] by John Sloan (1871–1951), painter, graphic artist, illustrator, and, for a short time, political cartoonist for the *Masses*. Upon receiving Henri's letter about Daumier, which was accompanied by examples of Daumier's work, Sloan replied: "I was ever so much pleased at your sending the Daumiers. They are fine and give me a feeling like tonic. He makes you see what he saw and knew was worth seeing."[31] In 1906 Sloan bought twelve volumes of *Charivari*, which contained almost 800 of the best of Daumier's prints. In his diary, Sloan wrote: "Spent the evening gloating over my Daumier lithographs."[32] In his teaching, he praised the beauty of Daumier's lithographs, his superb drawing style, and the humanity of his work:

Study Daumier's prints. His use of the medium is honest and handsome. He made thousands of lithographs and was able to keep the drawing alive and fresh. . . . The fact that men like Delacroix and Daumier were making illustrations seems to have something to do with the livingness of their prints. The medium was only incidental and they drew the best qualities out of it. . . .[33]

Don't be afraid to be human. Draw with human kindness, with appreciation for the marvel of existence. . . . Look at the work of Daumier.[34]

Sloan, Luks, and Glackens were assigned to do some illustrations for an edition of the collected works of Charles Paul de Kock, to be published in English by the Frederick Quinby Company of Boston.[35] Daumier, a contemporary of de Kock's, had made forty-four illustrations for *La Grande Ville: Nouveau Tableau de Paris*, de Kock's book about Parisian life. *Les Champs Elysées. Le Jeu de boules*, 1844 (Fig. 20), and *Révolution causée par une pluie d'orage. . .*, 1844 (Fig. 21), are two of these delightful works: the former illustrates how serious the game of *boule* is to its participants; the latter depicts the reactions of people to a sudden downpour. Sloan may not have seen these wood engravings, but he did immerse himself in Daumier's period and, from 1903 to 1905, produced fifty-three etchings for the series; Luks made three, Glackens fourteen.

In 1905 Sloan began his own lively etchings on urban existence, a group of works that became known as *New York City Life*. He wrote of that time: "Work on the de Kock illustrations . . . had fired my imagination and increased the technical skill in handling the etching needle. . . . New York had its human comedy and I felt like making pictures of this everyday world."[36] In the first etching, *Connoisseurs of Prints*, 1905 (Fig. 22), Sloan's purpose was to picture "some ideas of social commentary based on Hogarth's morality series or Daumier's dramatis personnae."[37] *Connoisseurs of Prints* satirizes the art pretensions of the upper classes. Telling comments on spectators at exhibitions were also made by Daumier in *Devant le Tableau de M. Manet. . .*, 1865 (Fig. 23), in which the viewers are lost and uncomprehending, and in *Devant les Tableaux de Meissonnier*, 1852 (Fig. 24), in which the spectators appear smug in the knowledge that they are in front of the "right" pictures.

Fig. 22. John Sloan, *Connoisseurs of Prints*, 1905, etching (M. 127). Kraushaar Galleries, New York.

Fig. 23. Honoré Daumier, *Devant le Tableau de M. Manet. . . ,* lithograph. *Le Charivari,* 19 June 1865 (D. 3446). The Metropolitan Museum of Art, Rogers Fund, 1922.

Fig. 24. Honoré Daumier, *Devant les Tableaux de Meissonnier,* lithograph. *Le Charivari,* 3 May 1852 (D. 2294). The Metropolitan Museum of Art, Gift of William Ivins, 1923.

Fig. 25. John Sloan, *The Show Case,* 1905, etching (M.129). Kraushaar Galleries, New York (Photo: Geoffrey Clements).

As indicated by *The Show Case*, 1905 (Fig. 25), Sloan soon began to lose interest in satirizing the upper classes. Here the well-to-do are relegated to the edge of the etching, and Sloan's joyous feeling for the vitality of life is pictured in the adolescents who are excited by the secrets of the *toilette* in a store window. Daumier had already drawn a similar subject in *Oh! p'pa . . . la belle femme! . . .*, 1846 (Fig. 26). In Daumier's work the father is upset at the hint of sex, but in Sloan's etching the haughty people seem to be upset by the rowdiness of the girls.

George Bellows (1882–1925), who had been on the art staff of the *Masses* from 1913 to 1917, combined his ability as a draftsman and his need to draw social or political statements with the technical freedom and coloristic qualities afforded by the lithographic medium. Beginning in 1916, he produced nearly 200 lithographs in his lifetime. He recognized that "lithography in its true sense (drawing on stone) offers opportunities for the artist greatly superior to any direct effort on paper. . . ,"[38] and he noted that the works of Daumier and Gavarni were "the great classic examples of this art."[39]

As early as 1908, Bellows had worked to make a careful copy of *Rue Transnonain*.[40] In 1916, he set up a lithographic workshop in his house and employed lithographic printers (George Miller in 1916; Bolton Brown in 1921) to produce his editions, just as the great master printer Lemercier had printed those of Daumier and Gavarni. The money he received from the sale of his lithographs climbed from $100 in 1916 to $1000 in 1921, a rise that may be attributed to the revival of lithography as a painter's medium, which owed much of its inspiration to Daumier.

Bellows' *Business-Men's Bath*, 1923 (Fig. 27), illustrates the same group of unlovely bodies trying to develop healthy physiques as Daumier's *On m'a conseillé les bains froids. . .*, 1858 (Fig. 28). Bellows' *Billy Sunday*, 1923 (Fig. 29), is a more intense and forceful reaction to a man Bellows considered a religious fanatic, but whose power, nevertheless, seems to have fascinated the artist. A commentator noted after Bellows' death that he was a "superb lithographic craftsman. . . whose explorations in the realm of social satire struck rather a new note in this country's art . . . [he] loved the clash and color of existence in the great cities. He saw dramatically and realistically. . . . Bellows was far more akin in spirit to Daumier, Toulouse-Lautrec, or to Forain, than to the artists of his own country, but not so penetrating as the French. America's acceptance of caricature in literature and art is recent."[41]

There were many other artist-commentators of the social comedy or of political events, but, because he tapped a vein of recognition, Daumier was singled out by the artists who

Fig. 26. Honoré Daumier: *Les Papas. Oh! p'pa . . . la belle femme! . . .*, lithograph. *Le Charivari*, 10 December 1846 (D. 1568). The Metropolitan Museum of Art, Bequest of Howard Carter, 1949.

Fig. 27. George Bellows, *Business-Men's Bath*, 1923, lithograph (M. 145; B. 125). Prints Division, The New York Public Library, Astor, Lenox and Tilden Foundations.

Fig. 28. Honoré Daumier, *On m'a conseillé les bains froids pour me faire maigrir! . . ./Tiens, et moi pour me faire engraisser! . . . il paraît que c'est bon pour tout cette année-ci! . . ./Oui . . . excepté pour se nettoyer! . . . ,*lithograph. *Le Charivari,* 2 August 1858 (D. 2874). Prints Division, The New York Public Library, Astor, Lenox and Tilden Foundations.

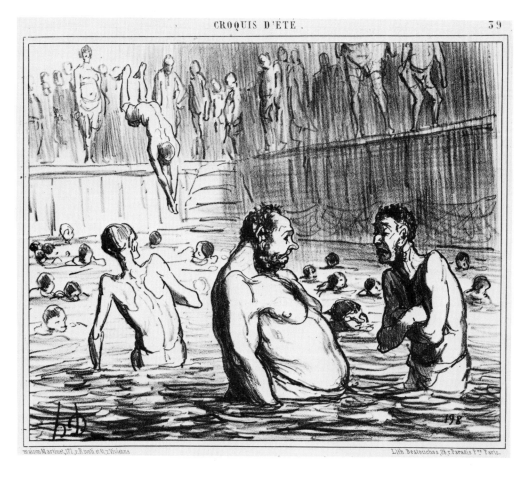

Fig. 29. George Bellows, *Billy Sunday*, 1923, lithograph (M. 143; B. 111). Prints Division, The New York Public Library, Astor, Lenox and Tilden Foundations.

came after him. Political artists took heart from his unswerving commitment to the people's cause and his attempts to sway the outcome of popular struggles. The realists admired his gift to depict truthfully the people of his time. Both kinds of artists were moved by Daumier's humanity, his compelling motifs and compositions, and, above all, his great artistic power.

Acknowledgment

I would like to thank Helen Farr Sloan for her invaluable information on John Sloan, and the staffs of the Tamiment Library, New York University, and the Prints Division of the New York Public Library for their patient help in locating hard-to-find documents.

Notes

1 Oliver Larkin, *Daumier: Man of His Time*, New York, 1966, pp. 218–220, and idem, *Daumier in His Time and Ours*, The Katherine Asher Engel Lectures, Smith College, Northampton, Mass., 1962, n.p.

2 Henry James, *Daumier, Caricaturist* (1893), London, 1954, pp. 1–2.

3 Ibid., pp. 3–4.

4 Robert Henri to John Sloan, Paris, November 1899, p. 2: ". . . their value is but three cents a piece—I paid that—three sous each for them," John Sloan Collection, Delaware Art Museum, Wilmington, Del.

5 William Ivins, "Daumier—The Man of His Time," *Prints and Books*, Cambridge, Mass., 1926, p. 275.

6 Mahonri Young, "Honoré Daumier," in *Honoré Daumier: Appreciations of His Life and Works* (The Phillips Publications 2), New York, 1922, p. 56.

7 Richard Muther, *The History of Modern Painting*, New York, 1907, II, p. 14.

8 Albert Bigelow Paine, *Thomas Nast: His Period and His Pictures*, Gloucester, Mass., 1904, p. 95.

9 William Welling, *Photography in America: The Formative Years 1839–1900*, New York, 1978, pp. 169–170.

10 W. E. B. Du Bois, *Black Reconstruction in America*, New York, 1935, p. 219.

11 James Parton, "Comic Art in the United States," *Harper's Monthly Magazine*, December 1875, p. 41.

12 Frank Weitenkampf, "The Making of Cartoons," *The New York Times*, 20 July 1890, p. 3.

13 Ralph E. Shikes, *The Indignant Eye*, Boston, 1969, p. 319.

14 Art Young, *Art Young: His Life and Times*, New York, 1939, p. 68.

15 Ibid., p. 6.

16 Ibid., p. 10.

17 Ibid., p. 191.
18 Ibid., pp. 226, 254.
19 Ibid., p. 8.
20 Albert Christ-Janer, *Boardman Robinson*, Chicago, 1946, pp. 57–58.
21 Ibid., p. 26 (quoted from "A Dozen of the Most Distinguished Illustrators," *Vanity Fair*, August 1915).
22 Larkin, 1966, pp. 48–49.
23 Frank Weitenkampf, "Notes on Women in American Caricature," *American Collector*, July 1946, p. 6.
24 Frank Jewett Mather, Jr., "Some American Realists," *Arts and Decoration*, November 1916, p. 13.
25 William Glackens, "The American Section: The National Art," *Arts and Decoration*, March 1913, pp. 159–160.
26 Henri to Sloan, pp. 2–3.
27 Quoted by Giles Edgeton, "The Younger American Painters: Are They Creating a National Art?" *The Craftsman*, February 1908, p. 524.
28 Robert Henri, *The Art Spirit*, Philadelphia, 1923, p. 185.
29 Many of these caricatures are in the John Sloan Collection, Delaware Art Museum, Wilmington, Del.
30 Van Wyck Brooks, *John Sloan: A Painter's Life*, New York, 1955, p. 16.
31 Sloan to Henri, Philadelphia, 14 February 1900, The Robert Henri Papers, Yale University, New Haven, Conn.
32 Entry of 30 September 1906, John Sloan's diary, unpublished, John Sloan Collection, Delaware Art Museum, Wilmington, Del.
33 John Sloan, *Gist of Art*, New Haven, 1939, p. 186.
34 Ibid., p. 106.
35 Peter Morse, *John Sloan's Prints: A Catalogue Raisonné of the Etchings, Lithographs, and Posters*, New Haven, 1969, pp. 64–65.
36 Helen Farr Sloan, ed., *John Sloan: New York Etchings*, New York, 1978, p. viii.
37 Ibid.
38 Lauris Mason, assisted by Joan Ludman, *The Lithographs of George Bellows: A Catalogue Raisonné*, New York, 1977, p. 24.
39 Ibid.
40 Charles H. Morgan, *George Bellows: Painter of America*, New York, 1965, p. 86.
41 Ruth Pielkova, "The Lithographs of George Bellows," *Arts and Decoration*, 2, 1928, pp. 412–413.

Francine Tyler is adjunct assistant professor of art history at New York University, School of Continuing Education. As guest curator, she recently organized the exhibition *The First American Painter-Etchers* for the Pratt Graphics Center, New York, and is currently preparing a book on that subject for Dover Press.

Ben Goldstein

Daumier's Spirit in American Art

olitically, the nineteenth century was for France a period in which democratic principles, through violent struggles, became embodied in political institutions. Twice, Daumier saw his country try and fail to establish democratic government; at the end of his life he welcomed her third, albeit unsuccessful, attempt. During this time, always the discerning recorder and critic, he composed a *comédie humaine*, inexhaustible in its range and richness and unsurpassed in the pictorial mastery that won him a popularity achieved by few artists during their lifetimes.

In 1845, Baudelaire wrote that Daumier's "lithographic and wood engravings evoke the idea of color. . . . He conveys color as he conveys thought. This is the strength of great art."[1] "We acknowledge only two men in Paris who draw as well as Delacroix. . . . The first is Daumier the caricaturist; the second Ingres. . . . Anyone who examines the matter slowly and carefully will see that these three kinds of drawings have this in common, that they say just what they mean to say. Daumier draws better, perhaps, than Delacroix, if you would prefer healthy, robust qualities. . . . What distinguished Daumier is his sureness of touch. He draws as the great masters draw."[2]

One hundred years later, Carl Zigrosser was to write in *Prints and Their Creators:* "Daumier has Rembrandt's deep feeling for humanity which he presented in the complete drama of humanity in the dress of the middle class in great detail, understanding and humor. He presented the bourgeois in its noblest aspect, the tireless fighter for political freedom against censorship, monarchical reaction, war, extreme exploitation, ecclesiastical obscurantism, police brutality, and the venality of the law. No heroics, no ideal figures, no search for the beautiful or the sublime, merely scenes and incidents of daily life, topical, factual, often have made these scenes live for all time. They are [as] fresh and pertinent today as they were the day they were published."[3]

Daumier the graphic artist overshadows and obscures Daumier's reputation as a painter and sculptor. The official world of art—established critics, Salon juries, academies, and museums—refused to acknowledge that a humorous sketch in a cheap newspaper could be a work of art. Writers, however, including Baudelaire and Champfleury, found these images—ludicrous deformations and intense, direct expressions of compassionate sympathy and bitter scorn—effective allies in their war against the deadly average, the unchangeable rules of drawing, the hard and fast distinction between the noble and the commonplace.[4] Van Gogh wrote of Daumier: "I remember being so very much impressed at the time by something so strong and manly in Daumier's conception that I thought it might be a good thing to feel in that way, and to overlook or to pass by many things, in order to concentrate oneself on things that furnish food for thought, and touch us as human beings much more than meadows or clouds."[5]

During the late 1800s, American artists traveled to the Continent for their art studies; there was, however, little contact with Daumier's work. Works by Sargent and Whistler, the most famous American artists of the period, are without evidence of Daumier's influence. Among the first American artists to recognize Daumier's importance were Henry James and Robert Henri. James, an expatriate who spent most of his adult life in Europe, published an article in 1890 in which he wrote of

Fig. 1. William Glackens, *Far from the Fresh Air Farm*,
carbon pencil and watercolor on board (25½ x 17½
in.). *Colliers*, 8 July 1911. Private collection. (Photo:
Kraushaar Galleries, New York [Geoffrey Clements]).

Fig. 2. Glenn Coleman, *The Election Night Bonfire*,
n.d., lithograph (15⅞ x 21¹/₁₆ in. [sheet]). Collection
of Whitney Museum of American Art, New York.

walking along the Seine in Paris and discovering half a dozen soiled, striking lithographs in a printshop window. Recognizing the work of Daumier torn from the pages of *Le Charivari*, he entered the shop and found himself surrounded by bulging portfolios. After examining the copious collection, James was convinced of Daumier's artistic stature.[6]

After returning to the United States from Paris in 1892, Henri taught in Philadelphia at the Philadelphia College for Women, and organized the Charcoal Club with his students John Sloan, William Glackens (Fig. 1), George Luks, and Everett Shinn. They painted under Henri's guidance and, working as artist-reporters for the Philadelphia newspapers, covered the daily events in the city, making rapid, accurate sketches. To this group, Henri championed the work of Daumier, for his own humanistic impulses echoed those of Daumier's. Known as The Eight, these artists spearheaded the break with academic and

romantic art, a major change of direction in American art. Their influence carried through the 1930s and 40s with both the New York realists and the social realists and started to wane only with the acceptance of abstract expressionism in the 1950s.

Around 1900 Henri moved to New York, where he taught at several schools, including the Art Students League and the Ferrer Center, founded by the anarchists Emma Goldman and Alexander Berkman. Among his students were Moses Soyer, Man Ray, Niles Spencer, Harry Wickey, William Gropper, and Robert Brackman. During his brief exile in the United States, Leon Trotsky also studied with Henri. "It will do well for you to look at Daumier's lithographs," Henri urged his students. "His fancy is free. His statement is assured."[7] The teacher spoke of Daumier's humanitarianism and the dramatic impact achieved through his use of light and shadow. While teaching at the New York School of Art (1902–09), Henri in-

Fig. 3. Guy Pène du Bois, *Opera*, 1907, crayon and pencil on paper (14⅞ x 12⅜ in.). Collection of Whitney Museum of American Art, New York.

Fig. 4. George Bellows, *Artists Judging Works of Art*, 1916, lithograph (14½ x 19 in.). Chapellier Galleries, Inc., New York (Photo: Walter Russell).

spired a number of young artists to record the life of the city: "Glenn Coleman painted New York with affection (Fig. 2); Guy Pène du Bois reflected upon its satirical nature (Fig. 3); George Bellows captured its vigorous side (Fig. 4); and Edward Hopper its loneliness."[8] Moses Soyer brought his work to Henri, who severely criticized some of his drawings for their academic and superficial cleverness and compared them with a drawing by Daumier in the *Liberator*. The criticism made a great impression on Soyer: "Elatedly I described to my brothers the encounter with Robert Henri. I must have succeeded in transmitting to them some of my enthusiasm for Henri's ideas, the meaning and importance of which I felt, rather than understood, for they listened eagerly and were greatly impressed. We pored long and studiously over the copy of the *Liberator* which I brought

home."[9] In their art, others who studied with Henri reflected Daumier's humanitarianism as well as his drawing methods. Among these artists were Yasuo Kuniyoshi, Eugene Speicher, Henry Glintemkamp, Maurice Becker, Randall Davey, Fletcher Martin, Nathaniel Pousette-Dart, Gropper, and Margery Ryerson.

John Sloan, who never traveled abroad, worked in the United States, contributing to magazines, doing book illustrations, and making etchings and paintings. His first introduction to Daumier may have taken place in late 1892, during his studies with Henri at the Charcoal Club. Sloan was proud of being the first of his "crowd" to have made a lithograph (1905).[10] He taught at the New York School of Art as a substitute for Henri in 1906, and was on the staff of the Art Students League from 1916 to 1938. Among his students were Alexander Cal-

Fig. 5. Reginald Marsh, *This is her first lynching*, drawing. *The New Yorker*, 8 September 1934. Drawing by Reginald Marsh; © 1934, 1962 The New Yorker Magazine, Inc.

der, Reginald Marsh (Figs. 5, 6), Peggy Bacon, Adolph Gottlieb, Don Freeman, Otto Soglow, and Carl Rose. Those whose drawing styles come closest to Daumier's are Marsh, Bacon, and Freeman.

Sloan (Fig. 7), members of The Eight, and several of Sloan's artist friends including Eugene Higgins, Jerome Myers, Bellows, Rockwell Kent, Rollin Kirby (Fig. 8), Boardman Robinson (Fig. 9), Robert Minor (Fig. 10), Stuart Davis, Coleman, Pène du Bois, Arthur Dove, Walt Kuhn, Walter Pach, and Art Young were responsive to the populist movement. They were known as the New York realists and their interest, as with Daumier, was in contemporary city life. "It is with the New York Realists that I began as a painter and later as writer," wrote Pène du Bois in his autobiography. "They were revolutionists themselves as Frenchmen like Daumier. They began to look at their fellow-man with naked eyes, to see past and through, to almost blow away our saccharine fog. They had no patience with escapists. . . . Here was life in the raw or nearly so, not trying to pretend. . . . Daumier will satirize a man not because he doesn't resemble a god, but because he tries to resemble one. . . . I think of Daumier's attitude toward mankind as that of a doting father. He was much more likely to pity than to censure. . . . He was too greatly enamored of form to bother about the eggshell surfaces of the merely pretty face. . . . His vision as Delacroix said, equalled Michelangelo in magnificence. It far surpassed the Italian's in human sympathy."[11]

Boardman Robinson also taught at the Art Students League, from 1919 to 1930, and later at Colorado Springs Fine Art Center and Michigan State University. Robinson, an ardent admirer of Daumier, wrote: "There was no false thing in him. He was a romantic, true; but he dealt structurally with that which he knew. . . . He went right at form, working as one does in modeling. His drawing came daily, directly, and hot off his mind. Here is an example where one cannot separate the man from the craft. Daumier was a great man. His drawing is frequently calligraphic, he seems to achieve the form and the symbol at the same time. He painted as a draftsman. There was no hiatus between his thought and his stone or canvas. Had the photographic process of reproduction not been developed to such an extent between the time of the death of Daumier and my early years as a newspaper cartoonist, it might have been better for me. I feel sorry that I did not make more lithographs."[12] Among Robinson's students were Arnold Blanch, Lamar Dodd, Adolph Dehn, and Concetta Scaravaglione.

Harry Wickey, who studied with Henri at the Ferrer Center, became a teacher in 1919. He, too, joined the Art Students League. Writing in

Fig. 6. Honoré Daumier, *Ecce Homo!* or *Nous Voulons Barabbas,* painting (63 x 49½ in.). (Photo: Prints Division, The New York Public Library, Astor, Lenox and Tilden Foundations).

Fig. 7. John Sloan, *Goldfish*,
1905, lithograph (10 x 14 in.).
Kraushaar Galleries,
New York.

Fig. 8. Rollin Kirby, *Gathering
Data for the Tennessee Trial*,
1925, crayon drawing.

Fig. 9. Boardman Robinson, *Louvain '14*, 1914, drawing (4 x 5 in.). Kraushaar Galleries, New York (Photo: Geoffrey Clements).

1941 of his teaching experience, he stated: "There are three stages in an artist's career; the childlike stage, the self-conscious stage preoccupied with the aesthetic values, and the final stage where with technique acquired in self-consciousness, one draws again naturally as a child. Daumier, Goya, Rembrandt are examples of artists who attained the final stage. I myself have as yet rarely achieved it. The graphic works by masters like Daumier and Rembrandt abound in examples of what can be accomplished by the use of line alone. Line in their work is never used intuitively, but always expressively. With such supreme masters the fundamental graphic tools are always used simply. It is sometimes a very good idea for the student to make a careful copy of a free and seemingly sketchy drawing by such masters as Daumier, Goya or Rembrandt, in order to truly comprehend what it means to draw simply and fully. Daumier achieved a full textural sense by means of sculptural drawing."[13] Harry Sternberg, Don Freeman (Fig. 11), and Philip Reisman, among others, studied with Wickey. Sternberg and Reisman became teachers and

Fig. 10. Robert Minor, *Army Medical Examiner: "At last a perfect soldier!,"* crayon drawing. *The Masses,* July 1916.

Fig. 11. Don Freeman, *Ladies of the Evening*, c. 1935, lithograph (5 x 10 in.). The Margo Feiden Galleries, New York.

Fig. 12. Philip Evergood, *No Peace with Fascism*, drawing. *Mainstream*, Fall 1947.

emphasized social and humanitarian concepts in their teaching.

Like Daumier, The Eight and the New York realists related to social unrest and "hard times." Those born early in the twentieth century reached their creative maturity during the Great Depression of the 1930s. Banks closed, strikes erupted across the country, government created the Works Progress Administration (WPA), and unions were organized, even one for artists. Philip Evergood (Fig. 12), Gropper, and Ben Shahn (Fig. 13) were among those who, in their work, responded to the times in realist and social terms; these artists were the leading social realists of the period. In their paintings, murals, and prints, their subject matter included strikes, the trial of Sacco and Vanzetti, the conditions of the poor and the minorities, and antifascist themes. Shahn wrote: "Art has roots in real life. It may work as bitterly as Goya, be partisan, as was Daumier . . . [or it may] discover the beauty within the sordid and real as did Toulouse-Lautrec."[14]

William Gropper's trenchant political drawings first appeared in the *Liberator* in 1918. His satire was sharp and his aim was directed against the leading domestic and international statesmen of the time. During the repressive period of the 1950s, he was summoned before a government investigating committee and questioned about his satiric drawings, as Daumier had been 120 years before. Like Daumier, Gropper was a painter, sculptor, and printmaker whose works, from 1920 to 1970, reflected the political scene in the United States, as had Daumier's in nineteenth-century France. A tribute from Lewis Mumford reads as follows: "In the mass, [Gropper's] paintings are a contrapuntal display of terror and delight, of horror and beauty, of misery and ecstasy, and they give Gropper a preeminent place as an interpreter of the mangled reality that people confront today"[15] (Fig. 14). Gropper's widow remarked that Daumier had been her husband's bible and God.[16]

Other artists of the period who dealt with subject matter closely related to that of Daumier include Aaron Bohrod, Howard Cook, Mable Dwight, Fritz Eichenberg, Freeman, Hugo Gellert, Harry Gottlieb, Lena Gurr, Robert Gwathmey, John Heliker, Joseph Hirsch, Jo Jones, Mervin Jules, John Koch, Kuniyoshi, Jacob Lawrence, Jack Levine, Martin Lewis, Louis Lozowick, Marsh, Elizabeth Olds, Anton Refregier, Ad Reinhardt, Reisman, Georges Schriber, Joseph Solman, Moses Soyer, Raphael Soyer, Sternberg, Lynd Ward, Charles White, and Grant Wood.

In a note to the author, Will Barnet (Fig. 15), popular contemporary artist and teacher, stated:

Fig. 13. Ben Shahn, *Man Washing Hands Against the Fence*, 1935, gouache (8½ x 5¾ in.). Kennedy Galleries, Inc., New York.

Fig. 14. William Gropper, *Critic*, oil (16 x 20 in.).
ACA Galleries, New York.

I was 14 when Daumier became my first great inspiration. His sense of form in portraying humanity appealed to my emotions and touched me deeply. Even in his smallest works there is a draftsmanship of bigness, which taught me the lesson that one did not have to paint the Sistine Chapel to achieve monumentality. His political cartoons are masterpieces of wit and satire which transcended the politics of the day. As with all his works, they are timeless.

It is always refreshing for me to introduce Daumier to my classes as an example of great draftsmanship. There is not a false stroke in his lines; each line defines the very essence of the individual character, its attire, and physical form. There is no need for contrived litho technique to cover up weak structure.[17]

Daumier's art also influenced the American political artist and cartoonist. In the first decade

Fig. 15. Will Barnet, *Fulton Fish Market*, 1934, lithograph (15½ x 11 in.). Associated American Artists, New York (Photo: Tracy Boyd).

Fig. 16. R. D. Fitzpatrick, *Yesterday—Lest we forget!*, 1939, crayon and ink drawing.

of the twentieth century, Rollin Kirby, Boardman Robinson, and Robert Minor incorporated the lithographic crayon technique into their repertoire, and worked with printing pressmen to make reproduction possible. The old pen-and-ink tradition of American cartooning gave way to a quick and restive style, the use of bulky shapes, and, through the use of crayon and pencil on grained paper, an economy of line. When asked if he considered editorial cartooning an art, Kirby replied: "Yes, indeed I do, when it is practised by a great artist like Daumier."[18] Political editorial cartoonists who carried on the tradition include R. Daniel Fitzpatrick (Fig. 16), Oscar Cesare, Gropper, Jacob Burck, Fred Ellis, and Herblock. Among the contemporary newspaper cartoonists are Bill Mauldin, Ollie Harrington, and David Levine (Fig. 17).

Daumier's conceptual and technical power may best be summed up by Mabel Dwight (Fig. 18) in her essay *Satire in Art:*

"Some artists (newspaper cartoonists) are very able and embody universal conceptions, and as life changes her dress often—but her disposition seldom. Certainly many of Daumier's newspaper drawings might have issued from this morning's press as far as their ideas are concerned, but his best work sheds enough radiance to light up everything he ever touched. He never copied nature; never drew from life. He looked at it with his mind's eye and abstracted meanings. He constantly trained his hand to obey his mind until his ideas flowed through his fingertips onto stone with unconscious fluency, as if conceiving an idea and drawing it were one single gesture. Daumier used distortion in his political caricature. Perhaps he wished to reveal the motives of men behind their facial masks and felt that the exaggeration focused attention on telltale characteristics. He was not concerned with their bodies. However, the body is just as revealing as the face. I feel that when Daumier was most truly the artist and revealer of character, his work was most free from deliberate distortion."[19]

The generation of artists who matured after World War II were not concerned with social realism. Abstract expressionism had become the dominant force in American art. Institutions, the press, collectors, and critics related to the technical and design needs of the artist. An-

Fig. 17. David Levine, *Untitled*, 1967, ink drawing. Reprinted with permission from the New York Review of Books © 1967.

Fig. 18. Mabel Dwight, *Brothers*, 1928, lithograph
(12⅜ x 9¾ in.). Weyhe Galleries, New York.

tonio Frasconi, Leon Golub, and Charles White, were among those who, in their work, dealt with war and social conditions. The pendulum has swung again, and now realism is "in," though without the humanistic concerns of Daumier.

Notes

1 Howard P. Vincent, *Daumier and His World*, Evanston, Ill., 1968, p. 157.
2 Oliver W. Larkin, *Daumier: Man of His Time*, New York, 1966, p. 73.
3 Carl Zigrosser, *Prints and Their Creators*, New York, 1974.
4 Larkin, p. 69.
5 Zigrosser, p. 73.
6 Henry James, "Daumier, Caricaturist," *Century Magazine*, 1890, 39, no. 3, p. 402.
7 Robert Henri, *The Art Spirit*, Philadelphia, 1923.
8 Bennard Perlman, *The Immortal Eight*, New York, 1962.
9 Carl Zigrosser, *The Artist in America*, New York, 1942.
10 *Goldfish*, 1905 (Peter Morse, *John Sloan's Prints: A Catalogue Raisonné of the Etchings, Lithographs, and Posters*, New Haven, 1969, pl. 133).
11 Guy Pène du Bois, *Artists Say the Silliest Things*, New York, 1940, pp. 81–82.
12 Boardman Robinson, *Albert Christ-Janer*, Chicago, 1946, p. 57.
13 Harry Wickey, *Thus Far*, New York, 1941.
14 *The Shape of Content—Ben Shahn Lectures*, Cambridge, Mass., 1956–57.
15 *The New Yorker*, 27 March 1937.
16 Ben Goldstein, telephone interview with Mrs. William Gropper, July 1979.
17 Barnet to Goldstein, September 1979.
18 Jerome Myers, *Artist in Manhattan*, New York, 1940.
19 Mabel Dwight, "Satire in Art," in Francis O'Connor, ed., *Art for the Millions, W.P.A., F.A.P.*, New York, 1973.

Ben Goldstein, a collector of social and historical art, has previously published an article in *Print Review*. Among other exhibitions, he has produced the following: *Civil Liberties—The Artists' Response; The Presidency: Irreverent and Relevant; The Butcher, the Baker, the Candlestick Maker: Images of Labor;* and *Daumier's Graphics.*

Martech Presses

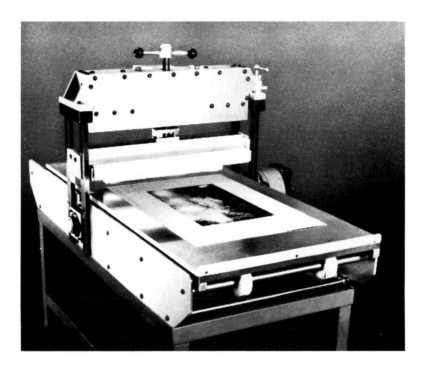

Litho Press

THE ALL NEW HYDRAULIC LITHO PRESS.

Fully automatic
Safe
Effortless
Maintenance free
Adjustable pressure
Excellent repeatability for superb printing
Standard sizes
24" X 48"
28" X 48"
32" X 50"

other sizes available

Can be seen at RYO Watanabe Studio in N.Y.C.   by appointment.

Write for brochure and price list:

Martech Etching Presses Ltd.
40-29 217 Street
Bayside, New York 11361
Phone: (212) 229-0485

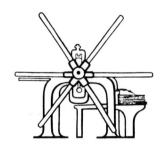

Honoré Daumier

1808-1879

A Centenary Tribute

an exhibition selected by Ben Goldstein and organized by Pratt Graphics Center with support from the New York State Council on the Arts

H.D.

Le passé.	Le présent.	L'Avenir
The Past.	The Present.	The Future.

Available at a modest rental through 1981.

Address inquiries to: Pratt Graphics Center, 160 Lexington Avenue, New York, N.Y. 10016

(212) 685-3169

Pratt Graphics Center
Circulating Exhibitions

The Pratt Graphics Center has prepared a number of exhibitions on the graphic arts for school, library, and museum galleries. The exhibits, organized under the direction of leading experts in the printmaking arts, are reflective of the expressive, diverse character of printmaking in the United States and abroad. All the exhibitions are ready for hanging. A modest fee is charged for each show. For a free catalog address inquiries to Circulating Exhibits, Pratt Graphics Center, 160 Lexington Avenue, New York, N.Y. 10016

Current Circulating Exhibits:

A Survey of Intaglio Printmaking
Photography in Printmaking
Eighth International Miniature Print Exhibition
The Presidency: Irreverent & Relevant
The Black Experience in Prints
The Figure and Machine in the Print Today
New Directions in Printmaking
Contemporary American Fine Arts Posters

Contemporary Serigraphs: The Silkscreen Print
The Collagraph: A New Print Medium
Printed Quilts / Quilted Prints
Funny? Four Centuries of Humor in Prints
19th Century American Trade Cards
Honorè Daumier: A Centenary Tribute
Images of Labor

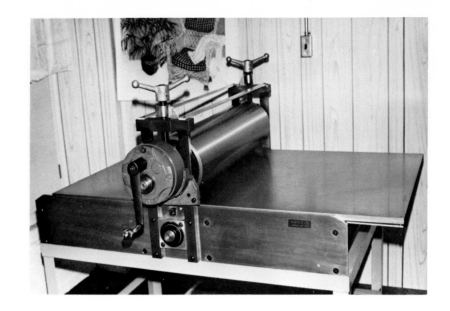

154

156

UKIYO-E
SOCIETY OF
AMERICA

An
association
of members
interested
in Japanese
Woodblock
Prints

For information write:

UKIYO-E SOCIETY OF AMERICA, INC.
1692 SECOND AVENUE,
NEW YORK, NEW YORK 1128

NEW EDITIONS
FROM PACE EDITIONS

STEPHEN ANTONAKOS
ETCHINGS

CHUCK CLOSE
ETCHING

AGNES DENES
LITHOGRAPHS

JIM DINE
ETCHINGS

JEAN DUBUFFET
SERIGRAPHS

LOUISE NEVELSON
CAST PAPER RELIEF

ERNEST TROVA
ETCHING

PACE EDITIONS
32 E 57   NEW YORK

❡ The distinguished artist, Fritz Eichenberg, is one of the world's foremost wood engravers. He is celebrated for his imaginative illustrations for *Tales of Edgar Allan Poe* as well as the novels, *Jane Eyre; Wuthering Heights; Crime and Punishment; The Brothers Karamazow,* and other classics of Russian literature.

❡ Avon Neal, poet, writer, and graphic artist, is best known for his creative rubbings of early New England gravestone carvings. His pioneering studies in other fields of folk art have resulted in the books, *Ephemeral Folk Figures;* the award-winning, *Molas: Folk Art of the Cuna Indians; Scarecrows;* and the highly acclaimed limited edition sets of portfolios, *Rubbings from Early American Stone Sculpture.*

❡ Hampshire Typothetae specializes in fine printing and was selected to produce this edition because of the meticulous attention given Fritz Eichenberg's engravings in the past. Harold McGrath, one of its founders, was long associated with Leonard Baskin's Gehenna Press and ranks among the finest letterpress printers in America today.

Pigs & Eagles

Avon Neal
Fritz Eichenberg

PIGS & EAGLES comes uniquely designed in two parts, each a separate entity, inserted together into a matching slipcase labeled on the spine.

❡ The first part contains a signed original wood engraving by Fritz Eichenberg conceived especially to illustrate Avon Neal's text. Cut on endgrain boxwood and carefully reproduced on Mohawk Vellum, the print is laid into an eight-page, hand-stitched wrapper and can be removed for framing and exhibition purposes.

❡ The second part consists of Avon Neal's powerful and timely ecological parable, a handsomely designed twenty-four-page book with sheets hand-sewn into heavy Strathmore Grandee cover stock. The text is meticulously printed using Centaur and Garamond types, illustrated with two details and the full wood engraving described above. Each copy is signed and numbered in the colophon.

❡ The book measures 8½ x 12 inches and is printed on a beautiful handmade, deckle edge paper manufactured in France, circa 1900, and expressly watermarked for Warren H. Colson of Boston.

❡ This edition, consisting of both the original print and illustrated parable, is limited to 500 copies and is priced at $65.00. Orders may be sent to:

Thistle Hill Press
North Brookfield
Massachusetts 01535

8th International Miniature Print Competition and Exhibition

ENTRY FORMS AVAILABLE: MAY 1, 1980
ENTRIES DUE: NOVEMBER 1, 1980
PRIZES AND AWARDS

Stan Washburn, *Decadent Bird,* Etching

Betty Davison, *Lazy Sunday,* Cast Paper Relief

Nancy L. Greco, *Three Wishes: One,* Lithograph

Georges Wenger, *Basilica de Guadalupe,* Etching

Exhibition: February 1981
Pratt Graphics Center
160 Lexington Avenue at 30th Street
New York, New York 10016

This exhibition will be available at a modest rental from April, 1981 through December, 1982.

Directory of Advertisers

Andrews/Nelson/Whitehead
Printmaking papers and lithographic stones
31-10 48th Avenue, Long Island City, N.Y. 11101
(212) 937-7100

Associated American Artists Inc.
America's largest collection of original prints
663 Fifth Avenue, New York, N.Y. 10022
(212) 755-4211

Jacques Barauch Gallery
Specialists—Eastern European Award Winning
Graphics. U.S. Representatives for Jiri Anderle and
Jan Saudek. Art Nouveau—major works by K. V.
Masek.
900 North Michigan Ave., Suite 605, Chicago, Ill.
60611
(312) 944-3377

Charles Brand Machinery, Inc.
Etching and litho presses, hot plates and large
diameter polyurethane rolloers.
84 East 10th Street, New York, N.Y. 10003
(212) 473-3661

Crestwood Paper Co., Inc.
Printmaking papers and museum mounting board.
315 Hudson Street, New York, N.Y. 10013
(212) 989-2700

Rudolph Faust, Inc.
Etching ink.
542 South Avenue East, Cranford, New Jersey 07016
(201) 276-6555   (212) 875-0556

Gallery of Graphic Arts, Ltd.
Contemporary Graphics & Framing
1603 York Avenue, New York, N.Y. 10028
(212) 988-4731

Graphic Chemical & Ink Company
Inks, tools, and supplies for the printmaker.
P.O. Box 27
728 North Yale Avenue, Villa Park, Illinois 60181
(312) 832-6004

Martha Jackson Graphics
Contemporary graphics by Appel, Calder, Hockney,
Johnson, Pond, Tapies, and many others.
521 West 57th Street, New York, N.Y. 10019
(212) 586-4200

Kennedy Galleries, Inc.
Old and modern master prints by European and
American artists.
40 West 57th Street, New York, N.Y. 10019
(212) 541-9600   Telex 14-8381

Kulicke Frames, Inc.
Complete selection of custom and standard-size
frames—metal, plastic, and wood.
636 Broadway, New York, N.Y. 10012
(212) 254-0140

L'Estampe Originale
Original prints, posters and rare books, 16th to the
20th century. Catalogues, lists available.
P.O. Box 897, Saratoga, Ca. 95070
(408) 867-0833

Martech Etching Presses, Ltd.
Etching & Litho Presses
40-29 217th Street, Bayside, N.Y. 11361
(212) 229-0485

New York Central Supply Co.
Retail art supplies
62 Third Avenue, New York, N.Y. 10003
(212) 473-7705

Original Print Collectors Group, Ltd.
International publishers and distributors of fine
signed limited-edition original prints.
120 East 56th Street, New York, N.Y. 10022
(212) 753-7929

Pace Editions Inc.
Prints by Dine, Nevelson, Dubuffet, Okada,
Youngerman; Multiples by Samaras and Trova.
32 East 57th Street, New York, N.Y. 10022
(212) 421-3237

Phillips
International auction rooms: Old Masters and
Modern Prints.
867 Madison Avenue, New York, N.Y. 10021
(212) 570-4845

Pratt Graphics Center Traveling Exhibits Program
Fifteen rental exhibits, catalog available.
160 Lexington Avenue, New York, N.Y. 10016
(212) 685-3169

The Purple Door
Original prints, fine and country antiques, bought
and sold.
1958 Post Road, Darien, Conn. 06820
(203) 655-4742

Daniel Smith Ink Co.
Manufacturers of fine printing inks; also suppliers of
presses, paper, and sundry items. Catalog available.
6500 32 N.W., Seattle, Wa. 98117
(206) 783-8263

Sotheby Parke Bernet, Inc.
Fine Art and Antiques Auction House
980 Madison Avenue, New York, N.Y. 10021
(212) 472-3400

Topal, Ind.Com.e. Imp.Ltda.
Presses. Etchings and engraving tools.
Catalog available.
Avenida Ipiranga, 879–Sala 13, Cep 01039–São
Paulo, Brazil
P.O. Box 1243; Telephone 33-7598

Ukiyo-e Society of America, Inc.
An association of members interested in
Japanese Woodblock prints.
1692 Second Avenue, New York, N.Y. 10028

Weyhe Gallery
Prints and drawings
794 Lexington Avenue
New York, N.Y. 10021
(212) 838-5478